FRANÇOIS TRUFFAUT

INTERVIEWS

CONVERSATIONS WITH FILMMAKERS SERIES
PETER BRUNETTE, GENERAL EDITOR

Photo courtesy Photofest

FRANÇOIS TRUFFAUT

INTERVIEWS

EDITED BY RONALD BERGAN

UNIVERSITY PRESS OF MISSISSIPPI/JACKSON

www.upress.state.ms.us

The University Press of Mississippi is a member of the Association of American
University Presses.

Copyright © 2008 by University Press of Mississippi
All rights reserved
Manufactured in the United States of America

First printing 2008
∞

Library of Congress Cataloging-in-Publication Data
François Truffaut : interviews / edited by Ronald Bergan.
    p. cm. — (Conversations with filmmakers series)
   Includes index.
   ISBN-13: 978-1-934110-13-3 (cloth : alk. paper)
   ISBN-10: 1-934110-13-2 (cloth : alk. paper)
   ISBN-13: 978-1-934110-14-0 (pbk. : alk. paper)
   ISBN-10: 1-934110-14-0 (pbk. : alk. paper) 1. Truffaut, François—Interviews.
2. Motion picture producers and directors—Interviews. I Bergan, Ronald.
   PN1998.3.T78A3 2008
   791.4302'33092—dc22
   [B]   2007024021

British Library Cataloging-in-Publication Data available

CONTENTS

INTRODUCTION

In 1992, 8 years after François Truffaut's death from a brain tumor at age 52, I sat in his comfortable armchair in his offices of Les Films du Carrosse, his production company in the rue Robert Estienne, a small street off the Champs Elysées. Although I'm not usually sentimental about such things, nor am I a believer in animism, I did feel a certain frisson as I sat where Truffaut had sat for many years, surrounded by his household gods. Posters from his films, and those of the directors he revered: Jean Renoir, Alfred Hitchcock, Roberto Rossellini, Howard Hawks, and Orson Welles. On one wall, there is a blown-up newspaper headline from his favorite film, *Citizen Kane*: "Kane Found With Singer in Love-Nest," and an enlarged *Peanuts* strip in which Lucie reveals the meaning of Rosebud to a frustrated Linus.

On his desk and on the mantelpiece above a fireplace, bric-à-brac of a certain significance and value to Truffaut. A stuffed bird from *Psycho*, a cigar box that belonged to Rossellini, an unfilmed script by Renoir. And on the shelves, hundreds of books, bold and defiant, the objects that Truffaut wanted to film in *Fahrenheit 451*, as he told *L'Express*, "burning as the burning of people. I don't say that I succeeded, but it was the plan to make a film about the importance of literature."

A quick glance at the shelves revealed Balzac's *La Comedie Humaine* and Flaubert's *Madame Bovary*. "My feeling [the love of literature] is expressed in that scene in *The 400 Blows* where Antoine lights a candle before the picture of Balzac," Truffaut explained. To Sanche de Gramont in the *New York Times Magazine* in 1969, he confessed: "I was very sensitive to the amorous intrigues of those around me, to the couples, to the adultery, so that when I read *Madame Bovary*, I identified with her completely, because she had money problems and so did I, and she secretly met her lover while I secretly went to the movies."

Naturally, among the books were all those that Truffaut had adapted for the screen: Ray Bradbury's *Fahrenheit 451*, signed by the author, and

Henri-Pierre Roché's *Jules et Jim* and *Deux Anglaises et le Continent* (*Two English Girls*), equally with a dedication to Truffaut; and the American "dime" novels: *Down There* by David Goodis (*Shoot the Piano Player*), *The Bride Wore Black* and *Waltz into Darkness* (*The Mississippi Mermaid*) by William Irish, *Such a Gorgeous Kid Like Me* by Henry Farrell, and *The Long Saturday Night* (*Confidentially Yours*) by Charles Williams.

When Charles Thomas Samuels asked why he usually adapts "trash novels to the screen," Truffaut replied "I have never used a trash novel or a book I did not admire . . . After seeing *Shoot the Piano Player* and liking it, Henry Miller was asked to write an introduction for a new edition of *Down There* and therefore had to read the book. He then phoned me to say that he suddenly realized that whereas my film was good, the book was even better. So you see, I don't film trash."

As much fiction as there was on the shelves, there were even more film books, including Truffaut's own *The Cinema According to Hitchcock*, in various editions and languages. Because of this lengthy interview book, which reads more like a dialogue (many of the questions are longer than the answers), Truffaut was continually being asked about his relationship to Hitchcock, both the man and his work.

It must be remembered that when Truffaut's book was first published in 1967, Hitchcock, in the twilight of his career, with his best work behind him, was greatly underrated, especially by American critics. Truffaut believed that his book had "succeeded in its primary task of making people revalue upwards the talents of a really great director."

Facing me, opposite the bookshelves, were rows and rows of video tapes, many of them taped by Truffaut himself, revealing his wide but selective taste. Apart from the directors already mentioned, there were films by Ernst Lubitsch, Max Ophuls, John Ford, Edgar Ulmer, Josef Von Sternberg, Erich von Stroheim, Billy Wilder, and Jacques Tourneur. I had the impression that I was ensconced in Truffaut's brain. And then I heard his voice . . .

No, it wasn't my imagination or in my mind's ear, it was really Truffaut's unmistakable voice coming from the television set in front of me. It was an interview he had given for French television on his idol Jean Renoir in the 1960s. I was brought back to the reason I was sitting in Truffaut's chair in the first place. I was researching my biography of Renoir, *Projections of Paradise*, and had been graciously welcomed into the inner sanctum by Madeleine Morgenstern, who had been married to Truffaut from 1957 to 1965, and who then ran Les Films du Carrosse (since sold, in 1999, to Marin Karmitz). Madeleine and François had remained close after their divorce, and Truffaut kept in constant contact with his two daughters, Laura and Eva, named after films by Otto Preminger and Joseph Losey respectively.

Les Films du Carrosse derived its name from the Renoir film, *Le Carrosse d'Or* (*The Golden Coach*): *The Mississippi Mermaid* is dedicated to Renoir, and the courtyard in *Bed and Board* refers to Renoir's *Le Crime de Monsieur Lange*. There are other examples of Renoir's influence as well as Hitchcock's, the two directors that Truffaut admired most and who come up most often in the interviews. Hitchcock, Truffaut felt, was able to portray the force of cinema by image alone, whereas for Renoir, words were more important. Truffaut once said that he wanted to film thrillers like Renoir, and tender stories like Hitchcock. But there were other mentors.

"Before I met Rossellini, I wanted to make films of course, but it see-med impossible. A dream. He made it all seem easy. He has a powerful gift for simplification. He told me, it isn't hard to write a screenplay, you only have to look at the reality around you . . . *The 400 Blows* owes a great deal to Rossellini" (Langley 1966).

On the other hand, in an interview with Peter Lennon of the *Manchester Guardian*, he says, "I think I'm closest to [Jacques] Demy—*The Umbrellas of Cherbourg*—in his aspect of playing a game. Making films is an escape from reality." This is one of the rare times Demy's name is mentioned—Truffaut was the younger by 8 months—but it makes sense when one thinks of the two directors' lightness of touch and their rejection of any documentary element in their work.

As is evident from his films and interviews, Truffaut was the most cinéphilic of all cinéastes, whom Sanche de Gramont calls "a member of a new species, the *homo cinematicus*, who is concerned—to the exclusion of nearly all other pursuits—with life at 24 frames a second." Perhaps his only equivalent in the USA is Martin Scorsese, who admits to being profoundly influenced by Truffaut. They shared a vast knowledge of cinema history, as well as a rapid way of speaking as if afraid of being interrupted. (Possibly something to do with their deprived and lonely childhoods, which drove them to seek solace in the cinema.)

"Are films more important than life?" asks Jean-Pierre Léaud in *Day for Night* (1973), Truffaut's loving tribute to filmmaking. For Truffaut the answer must be in the affirmative. For example, he explains that he didn't want to have a car accident while shooting *Jules and Jim*, "because I knew that the film was very complicated to cut so it was necessary for me to be alive until the final cut . . . I was in Finland when De Gaulle died . . . I said, 'I can't believe he's dead. He's busy writing his memoirs.' It truly makes no sense to die in the middle of work." In another interview he expressed how "when actors sometimes go skiing on Sundays . . . I'm sick all day with worry." When asked if he fears for the actors or the film, he replies, without hesitation, "For the film" (*L'Express* 1978; Petit and Glaessner 1973).

In contrast to directors such as John Ford, Howard Hawks, Raoul Walsh, who feel that their manhood is somehow threatened by too many questions and too much intellectualizing, Truffaut (like Scorsese) gave lots of interviews, as well as showing an obvious relish when speaking about other people's films he loved. Richard Eder in a *New York Times* article of 1981 (not in this collection) wrote of Truffaut: "He believes in interviews, just as he believes in cameras. Both are tools in a process that pleases him in a direct and uncomplicated manner— making films and having as many people as possible see them . . . He served fresh-squeezed orange juice, and his answers—considering there are no new questions to ask him—seem fresh-squeezed, too, and delivered with a pristine attentiveness."

For Charles Thomas Samuels, "Truffaut's quick lucidity made him the ideal interview subject. Even when he had to interrupt an answer to await translation (he speaks no English), he never lost the thread. Nor did he ever hesitate or appear to find any question unexpected."

What makes Truffaut rare among filmmakers is that he had been a film critic previously. Not just any film critic, but one who made a name for himself as a *provocateur* on the influential magazine *Cahiers du Cinéma* in the mid-1950s. It was Truffaut who first formulated the *politique des auteurs*, a view of film art that defended "true men of the cinema": Renoir, Jean Vigo, Hawks, Ford, and Welles, against the more literary tradition of the "*cinéma du papa*."

In 1957, in *Art*, another magazine for which he was a harsh critic, the 25-year-old Truffaut wrote:

> The film of tomorrow appears to me as even more personal than an individual and autobiographical novel, like a confession, or a diary. The young filmmakers will express themselves in the first person and will relate what has happened to them. It may be the story of their first love or their most recent; of their political awakening; the story of a trip, a sickness, their military service, their marriage, their last vacation . . . and it will be enjoyable because it will be true, and new . . . The film of tomorrow will not be directed by civil servants of the camera, but by artists for whom shooting a film constitutes a wonderful and thrilling adventure. The film of tomorrow will resemble the person who made it, and the number of spectators will be proportional to the number of friends the director has. The film of tomorrow will be an act of love.

This was two years before he started to practice what he preached.

Throughout his career as a director, Truffaut is continually asked about the effect of his having "changed sides," as it were. He answered in different ways: "Since I was a critic, I am perhaps less hostile to critics than other directors are. Nevertheless, I never consider the critic more than a single element in the reception of my films. The attitude of the public, publicity material, post-premiere ads: all these things are as important as critics." To the same interviewer he notes:

> One looks at films differently when one is a director or a critic. For example, though I have always loved *Citizen Kane*, I loved it in different ways at different stages of my career. When I saw it as a critic, I particularly admired the way the story is told . . . As a director I cared more about technique . . . Behaving like the ordinary spectator, one uses a film as if it were a drug; he is dazed by the motion and doesn't try to analyze. A critic, on the other hand (particularly one who works for a weekly, as I did), is forced to write summaries of films in fifteen lines. That forces one to apprehend the structure of a film and to rationalize his liking for it. (Samuels 1970)

Not only are his views on other films generally lucid, but he could be surprisingly objective (and negative!) about his own films. Naturally, the interviews Truffaut gave during or just after the making of a film are relatively upbeat, but when looking back from a distance of a few years, he sees faults. A few examples: "I'm no great admirer of my own film version of *Jules and Jim* (I'm pleased it has such a good reputation but it is not as good as its reputation)." He didn't think it was "physical" enough, and he was sorry that the idea of a *ménage á trois* alienated too many people. "I like the music in *The 400 Blows* and *Shoot the Piano Player* but am not crazy about the music in *Jules and Jim*. The music in *The Soft Skin* and *Fahrenheit 451* is excellent, less so in *The Bride Wore Black*. *Stolen Kisses* has a wonderful score, as does *The Wild Child*. But the score of *Mississippi Mermaid* isn't very good, and that in *Bed and Board* is simply awful" (Allen 1979; Samuels 1970).

But most interesting was his statement, in a wide-ranging interview he gave *L'Express* in 1978, that "the only film that I regret having made is *The Bride Wore Black*." The reason he gives is an ethical one. "An apology for idealistic vengeance shocks me in reality. When I saw Robert Enrico's *Le Vieux Fusil* (*The Old Gun*) I experienced a discomfort, but I did the same thing. One doesn't have the right to take vengeance. It is not noble. One betrays something in oneself if one exalts in it."

This may come as a shock to those who think of Truffaut as amoral and apolitical. But, his expressing distaste for the theme of *The Bride Wore Black*, is only an extension of his feeling uncomfortable with gangsters, uniforms, and politicians.

It was while making *Shoot the Piano Player* that "I realized I did not enjoy filming gangsters or violence. I found them boring. I didn't want to make heroes out of them or *Lavender Hill Mob* kind of inoffensive and funny gangsters, so I made my gangsters fantastic and promised myself—no more gangster movies" (de Gramont 1969).

Then when Truffaut was shooting *Fahrenheit 451*: "I discovered that I hated filming people in uniform—because, you remember, they were in the fire brigade uniforms, burning the books . . . Maybe the dislike of uniforms stems from my time in the army." As for politicians: "[They] do not deserve their star status. They should simply be modest and efficient charwomen" (Gow 1972; Allen 1979).

When asked by *L'Express* about his politics outside of films, he praised "the socialist monarchies of Scandinavia, because they seem to me countries which have attained real social justice." Truffaut said that he never voted. "I would feel I was performing a very artificial act if I voted, as if I were acting a part" (Allen 1979). Nevertheless, there is one occasion when Truffaut's involvement in politics had a significant effect, though it was, predictably, connected with cinema.

In February 1968, André Malraux, the former Communist and once great political novelist, now General De Gaulle's Minister of Culture, sacked Henri Langlois, the controversial head and co-founder of the Cinémathèque Française. This caused an uproar, and French and foreign filmmakers (including Truffaut, Jean Renoir, Jean-Luc Godard, Alain Resnais, Claude Chabrol, Robert Bresson, Georges Franju, Roberto Rossellini, Michelangelo Antonioni, Federico Fellini, and Ingmar Bergman) immediately announced that they would not permit the new administration to screen their films. The demonstrations outside the Cinémathèque at the Palais de Chaillot and in the streets, which brought out the riot police, was a prelude to the explosive events of May 1968. The Cinémathèque was closed down, and so was most film activity. (The opening shot of Truffaut's *Stolen Kisses* of 1968 is of the shut and barred entrance of the Cinémathèque.)

At the Cannes Film Festival in May, the French cinema's ruling body, *Etats Généraux du Cinéma*, adopted a motion demanding that the festival be cancelled. "We refuse to be of service to a brutal capitalist society which we put in question," it stated. The jury resigned and the festival was aborted.

In an interview, which appeared in the Autumn 1968 *Sight & Sound*, Truffaut explained his motives in leading the movement which stopped the Cannes Film Festival a few months before. Interviewed by Gilles Jacob who, some years later would become director of the Cannes Film Festival, he said, "I am not politically-minded and as a rule I try to steer clear of this kind of thing, but after what happened in February I wanted to see the end of this regime."

However, in stark contrast to the oeuvre of his erstwhile New Wave comrade, Jean-Luc Godard, Truffaut's films are not overtly political in any way. "For right or wrong, I believe there is no art without paradox: now in the political film, there is no paradox, because already in the script, it is decided who is good and who is bad . . ." (*L'Express* 1978).

Throughout the interviews, he stresses his abhorrence of "social cinema." "In some sort of way these films are traitors to cinema, they are theoretical demonstrations . . . I would not wish to be misunderstood on this point. I like realist films in the best sense, it is the 'social' film I

am against . . . We did not denounce for so many years what was artificial in the cinema of Cayatte to create all of a sudden a 'neo-Cayattism'!
That is what happened after 1968. One forced filmmakers to give in to
blackmail to sprinkle politics on stories that don't need it."

André Cayatte, still active in 1978 when Truffaut made the declaration above to *L'Express*, was the kind of didactic director that the young
critics on *Cahiers du Cinéma* had reacted against. Curiously and, some
might say, misguidedly, Antonioni also comes in for Truffaut's disdain.
"Antonioni is the only important director that I have nothing good to
say about. He bores me; he's so solemn and humorless . . . I don't see
the merit of so much gravity. In *Blow-Up* he was telling us, 'This is
England today.' Well, that is a topic for journalists; I don't think it's
very interesting for an artist to turn himself into a sociologist"
(de Gramont 1969).

Even in *The Last Metro* (1980), he eschews any didacticism. Truffaut
stated that the film fulfilled three of his ambitions: to recreate on film
the climate of the Occupation in Paris in 1942, to show the backstage life
of the theater, and to provide Catherine Deneuve with the role of a
responsible woman. "After '68, in Europe, politics were overestimated.
You kept hearing the slogan, 'everything is political'—which I find
absurd" (Insdorf 1981). In *The Last Metro*, the line is uttered by the Nazi
sympathizer as a justification for ridding France of the Jews. Despite this,
Truffaut tried to live by the Renoir credo of "everyone has his reasons."

When someone suggested that any of his films had social or political
significance, Truffaut would energetically rebuff such an "accusation."
"There is nothing social in my films. No, there were no social implications in the prison scenes in *The 400 Blows* . . . Even if there was social
criticism in the Bradbury book [*Fahrenheit 451*] there is none in my
film" (Lennon 1967). And to Yvonne Baby in 1962: ". . . in spite of its
'modern' appearance, the film [*Jules and Jim*] isn't polemical. Without
doubt, the young woman of *Jules and Jim* wants to live in the same
manner as a man but it is only a particularity of her character and not a
feminist attitude."

What worried him in 1978, 17 years after the film appeared, was that
"it gave the impression that I was going with the fashion to make a
feminist film." Catherine (Jeanne Moreau) "will be recuperated by feminism, independence, a woman's choice . . . the topical subject that

made me want to run away . . . I know that this attitude may appear unpleasant. Let's say that my refusal to go with the mode is so deep in me that it makes me want to make films that turn their backs on topical themes which, possibly, could interest me" (*L'Express* 1978).

Truffaut's rejection of current topics or fashions is not a conservative one, but the need to retain a freedom and purity of expression uncluttered by the *zeitgeist*. For him, the eternal theme of Love "is more important than social questions. It is the way to lead people to truth. There is more truth in sentimental relations than in social relations. There is more truth in the bedroom than in the office or the board room" (Eder 1981).

Truffaut said that "there are very few films I like outside films about love in one form or another," and claimed that he had about 30 films about love in his head and if someone proved to him that nine out of ten films made were about love, he would still say it wasn't too much. On more than one occasion, Truffaut opined that if you suggested to ten directors to make *The Bridge on the River Kwai*, you would get almost the same film from all of them. But if you suggested to them the subject of *Brief Encounter*, you would get ten different films. "To speak of love requires a greater gift and obliges one to go beyond the frame of just telling a story" (Baby 1968).

Love, in Truffaut's world, whether obsessional or exploratory, is the domain of women. "Men know nothing about love. They are always beginners. The heroine is always the stronger" (Eder 1981). But these adult films, or rather, films about adults, still preserve a certain childlike innocence best seen in his semi-autobiographical series of five films with Jean-Pierre Léaud as his alter-ego Antoine Doinel. These seemingly lightweight films hide the pain at the loss of youthful spontaneity, and the difficulties of male-female relationships.

There was an extraordinary rapport between Léaud and his mentor, which began with *The 400 Blows* (1959) and continued through almost 20 years as Antoine gets older, falls in love, marries, has a child, divorces, and finally becomes a writer (not a film director) in the last Doinel movie, *Love on the Run* (1978).

In a couple of interviews, Truffaut reveals what lay behind one of his most famous technical effects: the freeze frame at the end of *The 400 Blows* when the boy running towards the sea, which he had never seen, suddenly looks backward at the camera. He explains how the

much-imitated happy accident came about in most detail to Gordon
Gow in *Films and Filming* (1972).

As Truffaut told Charles Thomas Samuels, another famous scene
from *The 400 Blows*—the interview Antoine has with the unseen
psychiatrist, was the result of improvisation, with Léaud answering the
questions (put by Truffaut himself but later dubbed by an actress) with
whatever came into his mind.

What comes out clearly in the interviews are Truffaut's methods in
working with actors, though he objected strongly to the phrase "direction of actors." "I direct no one. I'm not a captain! I point them toward
what is good for them or for the film" (Insdorf 1981). It is this sympathy
with the actor and his improvisational approach that accounts partly
for the freewheeling nature of many of his films.

"I don't like the actors to arrive on the set knowing their dialogue by
heart. I want them to learn it in the heat of the moment. I think when
you're feverish, in the medical sense, of the word, you're much sharper,
and I want my films to give the impression they were made with a fever
of 104" (de Gramont 1969).

Truffaut admits to only ever having had trouble with one actor—Oskar
Werner in *Fahrenheit 451*. "For the last three weeks of shooting we didn't
say a word to each other," he told Sanche de Gramont. Always frank to
the point of indiscretion, Truffaut analyses his problems with Werner,
with whom he had worked harmoniously five years before on *Jules and
Jim*. (Strangely, Truffaut and Werner died within a few days of each other
in 1984.)

One of Truffaut's main complaints against Werner was that he refused
to play Montag, the hero of the film, more gently. Because Truffaut's characters "testify to human fragility," he was drawn to actors that show a certain weakness. "I could never have made a movie with Clark Gable or
John Wayne or an American-style hero . . . The trouble in the States is that
so many actors today come from television where they've been hired to
play G-men and spies. No one has replaced Jimmy Stewart or Spencer
Tracy or Cary Grant, those gentle, clear-eyed actors" (de Gramont 1969).

Which brings us to consider Truffaut's ambivalent attitude to
America and American films. Primarily, Truffaut believed that the best
American films were made under the studio system. "I don't think
Americans respond well to independent production. Where American

cinema was at its most unjust was with men of genius like Stroheim, Sternberg, Welles . . . but with middling good cinema it was at its best: people like Dassin and Preminger made their finest films for the studios, not when they became their own masters" (Langley 1966).

He was also concerned that the best directors were right-wing such as John Ford, "who votes Republican and who supports the 'American presence' in Vietnam . . . there have been awful left-wing Westerns. Americans are perhaps more gifted at exulting war than condemning it" (*L'Express* 1978).

Truffaut grew up in Paris during the German Occupation of his country, when all American films were banned. At the end of the war, the first Hollywood films he remembers seeing were George Cukor's *The Philadelphia Story* and W. S. Van Dyke's *Rage in Heaven*, the latter, a lurid melodrama starring Robert Montgomery, Ingrid Bergman, and George Sanders, being "the first American film to stimulate my imagination" (*Andy Warhol's Interview* magazine, 1976, not in this collection). But the turning point for him was *Citizen Kane*, which Truffaut reckons to have seen 27 times. "Certainly it wasn't typical of American cinema, but it had everything we love about Hollywood combined with everything we love about European cinema. It is an incredibly complete film" (Gow 1972).

Apart from Welles, Truffaut considered Howard Hawks, "the greatest cinematic intelligence among American directors . . . To be specific: Hawks made the three best Westerns (*Red River*, *The Big Sky*, and *Rio Bravo*), the two best aviation films (*Only Angels Have Wings* and *Air Force*), and the three best thrillers (*The Big Sleep*, *To Have and Have Not*, and *Scarface*)" (Samuels 1970).

This kind of answer often puzzles some of Truffaut's Anglo-Saxon interrogators who are rather dismissive of serious Gallic approaches to Hollywood cinema. In 1967, Peter Lennon in the *Manchester Guardian* wonders why "French film critics read such bizarre meanings into so many third-rate Hollywood films. Their recent reading of Raoul Walsh's old B weepy *The Man I Love* was a good example." Lennon goes on to question some of Truffaut's interpretations of Hitchcock, bewildered by the intellectual approach to a director much condescended to, an attitude that Truffaut did much to change.

And Charles Thomas Samuels says, "Like many American critics, I'm surprised by your admiration for Howard Hawks and John Ford. Would you explain why you like them?" Truffaut does explain with his usual eloquence.

On the question of whether he would ever work in America, Truffaut is generally consistent. To the *London Observer* in 1960: "There [Hollywood] the choice of subjects is a matter of money—Broadway successes, literary best-sellers. They won't take risks and they suspect all films made on a small subject. Directors are rarely free to work in their own way." To *L'Express* in 1978: "In France, it is not ridiculous to make a film without stars. I don't feel less well treated by the industry when I release a film played by unknowns. In America, I was made to feel the difference. I would be in the B league."

Truffaut was offered *Bobby Deerfield* starring Al Pacino and Marthe Keller, "but racing car driving bores me, mainly because of the noise." Then there was *Bonnie and Clyde*. "It was a good script, but not at all for me. It's strange to say, but I don't like gangsters."

Nevertheless, Truffaut did get a taste of Hollywood when he appeared as Claude Lacombe, the UN scientist in Steven Spielberg's *Close Encounters of the Third Kind* (1977), his experiences being amusingly related in the 1978 *L'Express* interview. Asked whether he liked the film, Truffaut was non-committal. "I can't say I'm interested in UFO's. I'm only interested in sentiments, love stories that may touch me. Meetings that one has in life are so mysterious and so difficult to succeed in that that is enough to satisfy my curiosity. There is science fiction everywhere . . ."

It was the first time he had acted in someone else's film other than his own, except for a couple of cameos. "From the start, I felt like an actor. I felt transformed. I could even say that I felt 'feminized,' with the different meanings that that has. I wanted Spielberg to be happy with my performance. I felt a certain pleasure in pleasing him."

What he found beautiful was the way the small children from Alabama who played the little green creatures, recognized each other even though they were disguised in their identical costumes. (*Close Encounters* was partly shot in Mobile, "a sad town on the Gulf of Mexico with a lot of poor quarters and empty shops.")

Although Truffaut thought that Spielberg made him smile too much, he agreed that "it wasn't a bad idea to have used me because of a certain credibility that I brought to the character." This is exactly what Truffaut brought to his three other leading roles in *The Wild Child*, *Day For Night*, and *The Green Room*, all of which he justifies in the interviews.

In a way, he played himself as a film director in *Day For Night*, at the center, holding everything and everybody together. In *The Green Room*, as a man obsessed with death, Truffaut felt, by playing the role he would make the film more personal, which he explained was like a letter written by hand instead of on a typewriter.

Because the role of Victor, the "wild child," was a very difficult one for a 12-year-old boy, he decided to play Dr. Jean Itard so that he would be able to control and shape the performance of Jean-Pierre Cargol as the boy. Although Truffaut only made four films directly involving children (including his debut 18-minute short *The Mischief Makers*), his reputation as a director of children remains strong, perhaps because Truffaut never lost contact with the child within himself. "I had suffered because I was an only child and I felt I was still close to the world of children; so I make *The 400 Blows* almost like a documentary" (de Gramont 1969).

For Truffaut, *The 400 Blows* dealt with a lack of tenderness, and *The Wild Child* with the lack of knowledge, which the doctor (Truffaut) means to compensate by being tough but tender. Claude Veillot in *L'Express* (1969) captures a moment of the affection that Truffaut inspires among children. "While Truffaut is talking, the small Jean-Pierre Cargol comes up to him and hugs him. Truffaut twists the boy's ear and pulls affectionately at his hair, calling him 'my flea.' And if the director moves away for a moment from the place of filming, it's not rare to hear the voice of the little actor shouting, 'Where are you, my Truffaut?' . . . The almost fanatical love that the small interpreter has for Truffaut, is the ultimate and just recompense for Truffaut's tenderness."

It was the same with Jean-Pierre Léaud. "I picked him from 60 children I interviewed. He wanted the part so badly; he had such vitality. I was thinking of a more introverted child, and I kept adapting the screenplay to suit him . . . People said we looked alike, and it may be true. And then, because we saw so much of each other, there was a mimetic thing" (de Gramont 1969).

Truffaut's work with children is exposed in great detail in his October 1976 interview with *Film Comment* about *Small Change*. When asked if he had made the film from "a child's point of view," it was easy for Truffaut to answer in the positive because he made it in collaboration with the pre-adolescent cast. "And to satisfy the children I made the film less cruel . . . when you tell a story to a child, they always want to find optimistic happy things in it."

To James Clarity (*New York Times*, September 1976: not in the collection): "Sometimes it is very difficult to direct children. You try something over and over and then have to let it go. But when it works, it's 10 times better than with an adult." Truffaut feels a director has a great responsibility to children, especially where the death of a child is concerned. "You should do it only if it's very important; you must have very good reasons. In Rossellini's film *Germany, Year Zero* there was a child who committed suicide. It was a very good film. And the same is true of Bresson's *Mouchette*."

Death was a subject that lingered in the background of Truffaut's life and films for some time. "I am convinced that the first scene of death shot by a director marks a stage in his career," he commented of his first death scene in *Shoot the Piano Player*. There were deaths in four of his subsequent films notably in *The Bride Wore Black*, with its multiple killings. "One cannot film death for 56 days without being affected" (Baby 1968).

But it took him until 1978, with *The Green Room*, to make Death, "rather the faithfulness to death," the subject of a film, a mere six years from his own demise. "I'm 46 and I've already started to be surrounded by those who have gone . . . From time to time, the people whom I have lost, I miss as if they have just died. Jean Cocteau for example. So I take one of his records and I listen to it. I listen to his voice in the morning in my bathroom. I miss him . . ." (*L'Express* 1978). According to Truffaut, the theme of *The Green Room* was the contradiction between the cult of death and the love of life, made more poignant in retrospect.

In Truffaut's case, where his life was an open book, it is inevitable that there is an autobiographical thread running through the series of interviews. We learn about his childhood, his fears, his loves and hates. But, most of all, his tastes and outspoken views on cinema such as his feeling that "the film that marks the beginning of the period of decadence in the cinema is the first James Bond—*Dr. No*. Until then the role of the cinema had been by and large to tell a story in the hope that the audience would believe it . . . For the first time throughout the world mass audiences were exposed to what amounts as a degradation of the art of cinema, a type of cinema which relates neither to life nor to any romantic tradition but only to other films and always by sending them up . . ." These remarks made to Don Allen (*Sight & Sound*, Autumn 1979) was Truffaut recognizing postmodernism before the concept became current in the 1980s.

The last films were a looking back. *Love on the Run*, the last of the Antoine Doinel series, contains footage from the earlier films; *The Last Metro* recalls the period of Truffaut's own childhood in Occupied Paris. As he told Tom Buckley in the *New York Times* in 1980 (not in the collection): "I had a short haircut . . . A German officer patted me on the head. My grandmother saw him do it, and she called from the window of our apartment, 'Come in here this minute. I'm going to give you a shampoo.'"

The Woman Next Door was a return to the theme of adultery, and Truffaut's final film, *Confidentially Yours*, was a further adaptation from an American dime novel, another raising of Truffaut's *chapeau* to Hitchcock, a love letter to Fanny Ardent, soon to be the mother of his third daughter, and an "attempt to recapture the mysterious, nocturnal, glittering atmosphere of those American comedy thrillers that used to enchant us" (*François Truffaut Letters*, Faber and Faber, 1989). However, the crucial aspect of the film was that it was shot in black and white.

In the same letter of 1982, quoted above, to the producer Gérard Lebovici, Truffaut attempts to make his case to have the film made in monochrome, underlining the words *black and white* seven times. In several interviews over the years, Truffaut was very vigorous in his condemnation of color, which had become more or less obligatory from 1960. Like Marnie, in Hitchcock's film, who screams, "Stop the colors!" Truffaut declared in 1978, "Color has done as much damage to cinema as television. It is necessary to fight against too much realism in the cinema, otherwise it's not an art . . . When all films were in black and white, very few were ugly even when they were lacking in artistic ambition. Now ugliness dominates. Eight films out of ten are as boring as watching a traffic jam." And a year later: "How wrong we were to think that color was an improvement and not a handicap. Color is the enemy" (*L'Express* 1978; Allen 1979).

When asked why all his films since *The Soft Skin* (1964), with one notable exception (*The Wild Child*), were shot in color, he replied,

"Because I can't do otherwise. Whatever the film, it is planned that it will be shown on television one day, and they only buy films in color" (*L'Express* 1978). Truffaut felt that, as in the 1940s, directors should have the chance to choose whether they want to use color or not. At least he was able to make one more film in black and white before he died.

Back in Truffaut's chair in his office, I was reminded of his eloquence and charm by watching his last ever appearance on television. It was on the book program *Apostrophes* on April 13, 1984, a few months before his untimely death. Truffaut, looking a little older and grayer, but still bubbling with enthusiasm, with a twinkle in his eye, spoke warmly of Hitchcock, and films in general with the childlike glee that can be discerned in many of the interviews that follow.

RB

CHRONOLOGY

1932   Born February 6 in Paris, France. Father, Roland Truffaut, an
        architect; his mother Janine de Monferrand, a secretary.
1946   After dropping out of school, works as a labourer. Borrows
        money to found a film society. Makes the aquaintance of
        André Bazin. Having run away from home, he is placed in a
        school for juvenile delinquents.
1950   Enlists in the army following an unhappy love affair.
        Stationed in Germany, he goes AWOL. Military prison. Bazin
        helps to get him released and discharged from the army. He
        lives for two years with Bazin and his wife.
1953   Joins *Cahiers du Cinéma* as a critic.
1954   Publication of his article "Une certain tendance du cinéma
        française." He directs his first film, *Une Visite*.
1957   Sets up his own production company, Les Films du Carrosse,
        named after Jean Renoir's *Le Carrosse d'Or* (*The Golden
        Coach*). Makes *Les Mistons* (*The Mischief Makers*). On October
        19, marries Madeleine Morgenstern.
1958   Death of his mentor André Bazin, one day after he starts
        shooting his first feature, the semi-autobiographical *Les
        Quatre Cents Coups* (*The Four Hundred Blows*).
1959   Truffaut wins the Best Director prize for *Les Quatre Cents
        Coups* at the Cannes Film Festival. Birth of his first child,
        Laura Truffaut.
1960   *Tirez sur le Pianiste* (*Shoot the Piano Player*), "a pastiche of the
        Hollywood B picture" according to Truffaut, is another success.
1961   *Jules et Jim* (*Jules and Jim*), an invigorating tale of friendship
        and love, opens to ecstatic reviews. Birth of second child,
        Eva Truffaut.
1964   Release of *La Peau Douce* (*The Soft Skin*).

1965   Divorces Madeleine Morgenstern.

1966   Although Truffaut speaks very little English, he makes
        Fahrenheit 451 in England, his first and only English-language
        film. He publishes *Le Cinéma Selon Hitchcock*, a series of inter-
        views with the master of suspense, one of Truffaut's favorite
        directors.

1967   *La Mariée Était en Noir* (*The Bride Wore Black*), starring Jeanne
        Moreau, is Truffaut's most direct homage to Hitchcock.

1968   Henri Langlois, the cofounder and director of the
        Cinémathèque Française, is sacked by the minister of culture,
        André Malraux. Truffaut organizes *Le Comité de Défense de la
        Cinématèque Française*. The opening shot of *Baisers Volés*
        (*Stolen Kisses*), the third film featuring Jean-Pierre Léaud as
        Antoine Doinel, Truffaut's alter-ego, is of the shut and barred
        entrance of the Cinémathèque. Truffaut heads a group that
        leads to the closing down of the Cannes Festival in the wake
        of the May uprisings.

1969   Two contrasting films are released, the thriller *La Sirène du
        Mississippi* (*Mississippi Mermaid*) and *L'Enfant Sauvage* (*The
        Wild Child*), based on a true case history, with Truffaut him-
        self in the role of the doctor.

1970   *Domicile Conjugal* (*Bed and Board*), the fourth of the Antoine
        Doinel romantic comedies, is released.

1971   Jean-Pierre Léaud in a different role is a Frenchman who falls
        in love with two English sisters in *Les Deux Anglaises et le
        Continent* (*Two English Girls*).

1972   *Une Belle Fille Comme Moi* (*Such a Gorgeous Kid Like Me*), a
        blend of American and French farce, was Truffaut's way of
        "sending myself up."

1973   *La Nuit Américaine* (*Day for Night*), Truffaut's exuberant cele-
        bration of movie-making, wins the Best Foreign Film Oscar.

1975   Truffaut shoots *L'Histoire d'Adèle H.* (*The Story of Adele H.*), a
        biography of Victor Hugo's daughter, on location in
        Guernsey and Dakar.

1976   Truffaut goes to the USA to play the role of a scientist in
        Steven Spielberg's *Close Encounters of the Third Kind*. Release
        of *L'Argent de Poche* (*Small Change*).

1977   *L'Homme Qui Aimait Les Femmes* (*The Man Who Loves Women*)
          is released, a title that could have applied to its director,
          famous for having love affairs with his leading ladies.

1978   *La Chambre Verte* (*The Green Room*), perhaps the director's dark-
          est film, tells of an obituary writer (Truffaut himself) obsessed
          by death, who makes a shrine to his dead wife.

1979   *L'Amour en Fuite* (*Love on the Run*) ends the cycle of five
          Antoine Doinel films that began with *Les Quatre Cents Coups*,
          20 years previously.

1980   *Le Dernier Métro* (*The Last Metro*) fulfilled three of Truffaut's
          ambitions, to re-create the climate of the Occupation, to
          show the backstage life of the theater, and to provide
          Catherine Deneuve with the role of a responsible woman.

1981   Truffaut makes *La Femme d'à Côté* (*The Woman Next Door*),
          the first of his two films with his lover Fanny Ardent.

1982   *Vivement Dimanche* (*Confidentially Yours*), a comedy thriller
          made in black and white to capture the style of 1940s
          Hollywood, turns out to be his last film.

1983   Birth of his daughter by Fanny Ardent.

1984   Dies of cancer on October 21, aged 52.

FILMOGRAPHY

1955
UNE VISITE (A VISIT)
Director: **François Truffaut**
Screenplay: **François Truffaut**
Cinematography: Jacques Rivette
Editing: Alain Resnais
Cast: Francis Cognany, Florence Doniol-Valcroze, Laura Mauri,
Jean-José Richer
16mm, B&W
8 minutes

1957
LES MISTONS (THE MISCHIEF MAKERS)
Les Films du Carrosse
Director: **François Truffaut**
Screenplay: Maurice Pons, **François Truffaut** (uncredited)
Music: Maurice Leroux
Cinematography: Jean Malige
Editing: Cécile Decugis
Cast: Gérard Blain, Bernadette Lafont, Bernadette Jouve
35mm, B&W
23 minutes

1958
UNE HISTOIRE D'EAU (THE STORY OF WATER)
Les Films de la Pléiade
Producer: Pierre Braunberger
Directors: **François Truffaut**, Jean-Luc Godard
Screenplay: **François Truffaut**, Jean-Luc Godard
Cinematography: Michel Latouche
Editing: Jean-Luc Godard
Cast: Jean-Claude Brialy, Caroline Dim

16mm, B&W
18 minutes

1959
LES QUATRE CENTS COUPS (THE 400 BLOWS)
Les Films du Carrosse
Producer: **François Truffaut**
Director: **François Truffaut**
Cinematography: Henri Decaë
Editing: Marie-Josèphe Yoyotte
Music: Jean Constantin
Cast: Jean-Pierre Léaud (Antoine Doinel), Claire Maurier (Gilberte Doinel), Albert Rémy (Julien Doinel), Guy Decomble (French teacher), Georges Flamant (M. Bigey), Patrick Auffay (René)
35mm, B&W
99 minutes

1960
TIREZ SUR LE PIANISTE (SHOOT THE PIANO PLAYER)
Les Films de la Pléiade
Producer: Pierre Braunberger
Director: **François Truffaut**
Screenplay: **François Truffaut** from the novel *Down There* by David Goodis
Cinematography: Raoul Coutard
Editing: Claudine Bouché, Cécile Decugis
Music: Georges Delerue
Cast: Charles Aznavour (Charlie Kohler/Edouard Saroyan), Marie Dubois (Léna), Nicole Berger (Thérèse Saroyan), Michèle Mercier (Clarisse), Serge Davri (Plyne), Claude Mansard (Momo), Albert Rémy (Chico Saroyan)
B&W
92 minutes

1961
JULES ET JIM (JULES AND JIM)
Les Films du Carrosse
Producer: **François Truffaut** (uncredited)
Director: **François Truffaut**

Screenplay: **François Truffaut** from the novel by Henri-Pierre Roché
Cinematography: Raoul Coutard
Editing: Claudine Bouché
Music: Georges Delerue
Production and Costume Design: Fred Capel (uncredited)
Cast: Jeanne Moreau (Catherine), Oscar Werner (Jules), Henri Serre
(Jim), Vanna Urbino (Gilberte), Boris Bassiak (Albert), Anny Nelsen
(Lucie), Sabine Haudepin (Sabine), Marie Dubois (Thérèse)
35mm, B&W
105 minutes

1962
ANTOINE ET COLETTE (episode in *L'Amour a Vingt Ans/Love at Twenty*)
20th Century–Fox (Distributor)
Producer: Pierre Roustang
Director: **François Truffaut**
Screenplay: **François Truffaut**
Cinematography: Raoul Coutard
Editing: Claudine Bouché
Music: Georges Delerue
Cast: Jean-Pierre Léaud (Antoine Doinel), Marie-France Pisier (Colette),
Patrick Auffay (René), Rosy Varte (Colette's mother)
35mm, B&W
30 minutes

1964
LA PEAU DOUCE (THE SOFT SKIN)
Les Films du Carrosse
Producers: António da Cunha Telles (uncredited), **François Truffaut**
(uncredited)
Director: **François Truffaut**
Screenplay: **François Truffaut**, Jean-Louis Richard
Cinematography: Raoul Coutard
Editing: Claudine Bouché
Music: Georges Delerue
Cast: Jean Desailly (Pierre Lachenay), Françoise Dorléac (Nicole), Nelly
Benedetti (Franca Lachenay), Daniel Ceccaldi (Clément), Laurence
Badie (Ingrid), Sabine Haudepin (Sabine Lachenay)

35mm, B&W
113 minutes

1966
FAHRENHEIT 451
Anglo Enterprises, Vineyard Film Limited
Producer: Lewis M. Allen
Director: **François Truffaut**
Screenplay: **François Truffaut**, Jean-Louis Richard from the novel of the
same name by Ray Bradbury
Cinematography: Nicolas Roeg
Editing: Thom Noble
Music: Bernard Herrmann
Production Design: Syd Cain, Tony Walton
Cast: Oskar Werner (Guy Montag), Julie Christie (Clarisse/Linda
Montag), Cyril Cusack (The Captain), Anton Diffring (Fabian), Jeremy
Spense (Man with the Apple), Bee Duffell (Book Lady)
35mm, Color
112 minutes

1967
LA MARIÉE ÉTAIT EN NOIR (THE BRIDE WORE BLACK)
Dino de Laurentiis Cinematografica, Les Films du Carrosse,
Les Productions Artistes Associés
Producers: Marcel Bebert (uncredited), Oscar Lewenstein (uncredited)
Director: **François Truffaut**
Screenplay: **François Truffaut**, Jean-Louis Richard from the novel
The Bride Wore Black by William Irish (Cornell Woolrich)
Cinematography: Raoul Coutard
Editing: Claudine Bouché
Music: Bernard Herrmann
Production Design: Pierre Guffroy
Cast: Jeanne Moreau (Julie Kohler), Michel Bouquet (Coral), Jean-
Claude Brialy (Corey), Charles Denner (Fergus), Claude Rich (Bliss),
Michael Lonsdale (Rene Morane), Daniel Boulanger (Delvaux),
Alexandra Stewart (Mlle Becker)
35mm, Color
107 minutes

1968
BAISERS VOLÉS (STOLEN KISSES)
Les Films du Carrosse, Les Productions Artistes Associés
Producers: Marcel Bebert (uncredited), **François Truffaut** (uncredited)
Director: **François Truffaut**
Screenplay: **François Truffaut**, Claude de Givray, Bernard Revon
Cinematography: Denys Clerval
Editing: Agnès Guillemot
Music: Antoine Duhamel
Production Design: Claude Pignot
Cast: Jean-Pierre Léaud (Antoine Doinel), Delphine Seyrig (Fabienne
Tabard), Claude Jade (Christine Darbon), Michael Lonsdale (Georges
Tabard), Harry-Max (Monsieur Henri), André Falcon (Monsieur Blady),
Daniel Ceccaldi (Monsieur Darbon), Claire Duhamel (Madame Darbon)
35mm, Color
90 minutes

1969
LA SIRÈNE DU MISSISSIPPI (MISSISSIPPI MERMAID)
Les Films du Carrosse, Les Productions Artistes Associés
Producers: Marcel Berbert, **François Truffaut**
Director: **François Truffaut**
Screenplay: **François Truffaut** from the novel *Waltz into Darkness*
by William Irish (Cornell Woolrich)
Cinematography: Denys Clerval
Editing: Agnès Guillemot
Music: Antoine Duhamel
Production Design: Claude Pignot
Cast: Jean-Paul Belmondo (Louis Mahé), Catherine Deneuve (Julie
Roussel/Marion Vergano), Nelly Borgeaud (Berthe), Martine Ferrière
(Landlady), Marcel Berbert (Jardine), Yves Drouhet (Detective),
Michel Bouquet (Camolli)
35mm, Color
123 minutes

1970
L'ENFANT SAUVAGE (THE WILD CHILD)
Les Films du Carrosse, Les Productions Artistes Associés

Producer: Marcel Berbert
Director: **François Truffaut**
Screenplay: **François Truffaut**, Jean Gruault from the novel *Mémoires et rapport sur Victor de l'Aveyron* by Jean Itard
Cinematography: Nestor Almendros
Editing: Agnès Guillemot
Music: Antonio Vivaldi
Production Design: Jean Mandaroux
Cast: Jean-Pierre Cargol (Victor), **François Truffaut** (Dr. Jean Itard), Françoise Seigner (Madame Guerin), Jean Dasté (Professor Philippe Pinel), Annie Miller (Madame Lemeri), Claude Miller (Monsieur Lemeri)
35mm, B&W
83 minutes

1970
DOMICILE CONJUGAL (BED AND BOARD)
Les Films du Carrosse, Valoria Films, Fida Cinematografica
Producers: Marcel Berbert, **François Truffaut** (uncredited)
Director: **François Truffaut**
Screenplay: **François Truffaut**, Claude de Givray, Bernard Revon
Cinematography: Nestor Almendros
Editing: Agnès Guillemot
Music: Antoine Duhamel
Production Design: Jean Manderoux (uncredited)
Cast: Jean-Pierre Léaud (Antoine Doinel), Claude Jade (Christine Darbon Doinel), Hiroko Berghauer (Kyoko), Barbara Laage (Monique), Danièle Girard (Ginette), Daniel Ceccaldi (Monsieur Darbon), Claire Duhamel (Madame Darbon)
35mm, Color
97 minutes

1971
LES DEUX ANGLAISES ET LE CONTINENT (TWO ENGLISH GIRLS)
Films du Carrosse/Cinétel/Simar
Producer: Maurice Berbert
Director: **François Truffaut**
Screenplay: **François Truffaut**, Jean Gruault from the novel of the same name by Henri-Pierre Roché

Cinematography: Nestor Almendros
Editing: Martine Barraqué, Yann Dedet
Music: Georges Delerue
Production Design: Michel de Broin
Cast: Jean-Pierre Léaud (Claude Roc), Kika Markham (Ann Brown), Stacey Tendeter (Muriel Brown), Sylvia Marriott (Mrs. Brown), Marie Mansart (Madame Roc), Philippe Léotard (Diurka), Irène Tunc (Ruta)
35mm, Color
108 minutes

1972
UNE BELLE FILLE COMME MOI (SUCH A GORGEOUS KID LIKE ME)
Films du Carrosse/Columbia
Producer: Marcel Berbert
Director: **François Truffaut**
Screenplay: **François Truffaut**, Jean-Loup Dabardie from the novel *Such a Gorgeous Kid Like Me* by Henry Farrell
Cinematography: Pierre William Glenn
Editing: Yann Dedet
Music: Georges Delerue
Production Design: Jean-Pierre Kohut-Svelko
Cast: Bernadette Lafont (Camille Bliss), Claude Brasseur (Maître Murene), Charles Denner (Arthur), Guy Marchand (Roger, aka Sam Golden), André Dussollier (Stanislas Prévine), Anne Kreis (Hélène), Philippe Léotard (Clovis Bliss)
35mm, Color
98 minutes

1973
LA NUIT AMÉRICAINE (DAY FOR NIGHT)
Les Films du Carrosse/PECF/PIC
Producer: Maurice Berbert
Director: **François Truffaut**
Screenplay: **François Truffaut**, Jean-Louis Richard, Suzanne Schiffman
Cinematography: Pierre-William Glenn
Editing: Martine Barraqué, Yann Dedet
Music: Georges Delerue
Production Design: Damien Lanfranchi

Cast: Jacqueline Bisset (Julie), Valentina Cortese (Severine), Dani (Liliane), Alexandra Stewart (Stacey), Jean-Pierre Aumont (Alexandre), Jean Champion (Bertrand), Jean-Pierre Léaud (Alphonse), **François Truffaut** (Ferrand), Nike Arrighi (Odile), Nathalie Baye (Joelle)
35mm, Color
115 minutes

1975
L'HISTOIRE D'ADÈLE H. (THE STORY OF ADELE H.)
Les Films du Carrosse/Les Productions Artistes Associés
Producers: Maurice Berbert, Claude Miller, **François Truffaut** (uncredited)
Director: **François Truffaut**
Screenplay: **François Truffaut**, Jean Gruault, Suzanne Schiffman
Cinematography: Nestor Almendros
Editing: Martine Barraqué, Yann Dedet, Jean Gargonne, Michèle Neny, Muriel Zeleny
Music: Maurice Jaubert
Production Design: Jean-Pierre Kohut-Svelko
Cast: Isabelle Adjani (Adèle Hugo a.k.a. Adèle Lewry), Bruce Robinson (Lt. Albert Pinson), Sylvia Marriot (Mrs. Saunders), Joseph Blatchley (The Bookseller), Ivry Gitlis (Hypnotist), Louise Bourdet (Victor Hugo's servant), Cecil De Sausmarez (Mr. Lenoir)
35mm, Color
98 minutes

1976
L'ARGENT DE POCHE (SMALL CHANGE)
Les Films du Carrosse/Les Productions Artistes Associés
Producer: **François Truffaut** (uncredited)
Director: **François Truffaut**
Screenplay: **François Truffaut**, Suzanne Schiffman
Cinematography: Pierre William Glenn
Editing: Yann Dedet
Music: Maurice Jaubert
Production Design: Jean-Pierre Kohut-Svelko
Cast: Nicole Félix (Grégory's mother), Chantal Mercier (Chantal Petit, the Schoolteacher), Jean-François Stévenin (Jean-François Richet,

the Schoolteacher), Virginie Thévenet (Lydie Richet), Tania Torrens
(Nadine Riffle), René Barnerias (Monsieur Desmouceaux, Patrick's
father), Katy Carayon (Sylvie's Mother), Jean-Marie Carayon
(Police inspector, Sylvie's father)
35mm, Color
105 minutes

1977
L'HOMME QUI AIMAIT LES FEMMES (THE MAN WHO LOVED
WOMEN)
Les Films du Carrosse/Les Productions Artistes Associés
Producers: Maurice Berbert (uncredited), **François Truffaut** (uncredited)
Director: **François Truffaut**
Screenplay: **François Truffaut**, Michel Fermaud, Suzanne Schiffman
Cinematography: Nestor Almendros
Editing: Martine Barraqué
Music: Maurice Jaubert
Production Design: Jean-Pierre Kohut-Svelko
Cast: Charles Denner (Bertrand Morane), Brigitte Fossey
(Geneviève Bigey), Nelly Borgeaud (Delphine Grezel), Geneviève
Fontanel (Hélène), Leslie Caron (Véra), Nathalie Baye (Martine
Desdoits), Valérie Bonnie (Fabienne), Jean Dasté (Docteur Bicard)
35mm, Color
120 minutes

1978
LA CHAMBRE VERTE (THE GREEN ROOM)
Les Films du Carrosse/Les Productions Artistes Associés
Producer: **François Truffaut**
Director: **François Truffaut**
Screenplay: **François Truffaut**, Jean Gruault from the novella
The Altar of the Dead by Henry James
Cinematography: Nestor Almendros
Editing: Martine Barraqué
Music: Maurice Jaubert
Production Design: Jean-Pierre Kohut-Svelko
Cast: **François Truffaut** (Julien Davenne), Nathalie Baye (Cecilia
Mandel), Jean Dasté (Bernard Humbert), Patrick Maléon (Georges),

Jeanne Lobre (Mme Rambaud), Antoine Vitez (Bishop's secretary),
Jean-Pierre Moulin (Gerard Mazet)
35mm, Color
94 minutes

1979
L'AMOUR EN FUITE (LOVE ON THE RUN)
Les Films du Carrosse
Producer: **François Truffaut**
Director: **François Truffaut**
Screenplay: **François Truffaut**, Marie-France Pisier, Jean Aurel,
Suzanne Schiffman
Cinematography: Nestor Almendros
Editing: Martine Barraqué
Music: Georges Delerue
Production Design: Jean-Pierre Kohut-Svelko
Cast: Jean-Pierre Léaud (Antoine Doinel), Marie-France Pisier (Colette
Tazzi), Claude Jade (Christine Doinel), Dani (Liliane), Dorothée (Sabine
Barnerias), Daniel Mesguich (Xavier Barnerias), Julien Bertheau
(Monsieur Lucien)
35mm, Color
94 minutes

1980
LE DERNIER MÉTRO (THE LAST METRO)
Les Films du Carrosse/SEDIF/T.F.1/SFP
Producer: **François Truffaut** (uncredited)
Director: **François Truffaut**
Screenplay: **François Truffaut**, Suzanne Schiffman, Jean-Claude
Grumberg
Cinematography: Nestor Almendros
Editing: Martine Barraqué
Music: George Delerue
Production Design: Jean-Pierre Kohut-Svelko
Cast: Catherine Deneuve (Marion Steiner), Gérard Depardieu (Bernard
Granger), Jean Poiret (Jean-Loup Cottins), Andréa Ferréol (Arlette
Guillaume), Paulette Dubost (Germaine Fabre), Jean-Louis Richard
(Daxiat), Maurice Risch (Raymond Boursier), Sabine Haudepin
(Nadine Marsac), Heinz Bennent (Lucas Steiner)

35mm, Color
131 minutes

1981
LA FEMME D'À CÔTÉ (THE WOMAN NEXT DOOR)
Les Films du Carrosse/TFI
Producer: **François Truffaut**
Director: **François Truffaut**
Screenplay: **François Truffaut**, Suzanne Schiffman, Jean Aurel
Cinematography: William Lubtchansky
Editing: Martine Barraqué
Music: Georges Delerue
Production Design: Jean-Pierre Kohut-Svelko
Cast: Gérard Depardieu (Bernard Coudray), Fanny Ardant (Mathilde
Bauchard), Henri Garcin (Philippe Bauchard), Michèle Baumgartner
(Arlette Coudray), Roger Van Hool (Roland Duguet), Véronique Silver
(Madame Odile Jouve)
35mm, Color
106 minutes

1984
VIVEMENT DIMANCHE (*Confidentially Yours*)
Les Films du Carrosse/A2/Soprofilms
Producers: Armand Barbault, **François Truffaut**
Director: **François Truffaut**
Screenplay: **François Truffaut**, Suzanne Schiffman, Jean Aurel
from the novel *The Long Saturday Night* by Charles Williams
Cinematography: Nestor Almendros
Editing: Martine Barraqué
Music: Georges Delerue
Production Design: Hilton McConnico
Cast: Fanny Ardant (Barbara Becker), Jean-Louis Trintignant (Julien
Vercel), Jean-Pierre Kalfon (Massoulier), Philippe Laudenbach (Maitre
Clement), Philippe Morier-Genoud (Supt. Santelli), Xavier Saint-Macary
(Bertrand Fabre), Jean-Louis Richard (Louison)
35mm, B&W
110 minutes

FRANÇOIS TRUFFAUT

INTERVIEWS

Crest of the New Wave

LOUIS MARCORELLES/1960

JUST BEFORE MEETING François Truffaut, whose film *The 400 Blows* won him the prize for direction at the last Cannes Festival and who is the most typical representative of the movement in the French cinema that has been labeled *la nouvelle vague*, I was able to learn what two of the most celebrated men in Hollywood thought of his work: they were Gregory Peck and the producer Sam Spiegel (*The Bridge on the River Kwai*), both on their way through Paris.

Mr. Peck thought Truffaut's film shapeless and lacking a subject: he believes that the cinema's aim is to deliver its message without any sacrifice at the box office. Mr. Spiegel, on the other hand, admires the film unreservedly, though he thinks its place in the commercial cinema is only marginal. For him, as for Mr. Peck, the art of the cinema is primarily that of the producer, who controls the work down to its smallest detail.

American Films

François Truffaut, on his return from a brief visit to New York, where he received the American Critics Prize, stated his belief in the dominant importance of the director. He feels he would not be able to work within the Hollywood system. "There the choice of subjects is a matter of money—Broadway successes, literary best-sellers. They won't take risks and they suspect all films made on a small subject. Directors are

From the *Observer* (London), 13 March 1960. © Guardian News & Media Limited, 1960. Reprinted by permission.

rarely free to work in their own way. But, having said that, let me say that I'm passionately fond of the American cinema. For many young French directors it's a model we strive to learn from: we admire its narrative speed, its general efficiency, and the restraint of its actors. Cinema addicts love American films, even the most idiotic ones; there's always more feeling in them than in ours. We tend to be too cerebral. But we ought not to copy Hollywood; you should never copy what you admire, especially when it's something remote from you."

The success of *The 400 Blows*, at Cannes in 1959 and then in the world at large, came as something of a surprise to Truffaut. "After all, it was a film made on a very small budget, with which I had taken a great many risks, and I was terrified of what the result would be. Even now after the reception it has had in Paris, New York, and London, I'm not convinced that my film really is popular."

"In New York I was particularly struck by the seriousness of American criticism. There's no French equivalent to it. American critics feel a great responsibility for the fortunes of foreign films, and they make a real effort to put all elements of the problem before their readers. I wouldn't say so much for their colleagues in France, where snobbery and dilettantism are the rule." Before he became an avant-garde filmmaker, Truffaut was one of the most savage of French cinema critics.

Today he wants above all to avoid the kind of official director's career which in the past he used to attack. "I have nothing against films made on large budgets. I'd be delighted for instance to shoot a Balzac novel in costume with fifteen different sets. But the first thing is to hold on to complete freedom. To begin with I thought of shooting my second film, *Shoot the Piano Player*, in studio conditions. But the cost of the production would have been trebled. In the end I decided to work on a very small budget, as I did for *The 400 Blows* and to shoot it entirely on location.

"The subject is freely adapted from an American crime novel by David Goodis, and the setting moved from San Francisco to Paris. It's about the life of a broken-down musician who used to be a celebrity and is now reduced to playing the piano in a bar. There isn't much story to tell. I have tried to give a portrait of a timid man, divided between society and his art, and to show his relationship with three women. But no treatise, no message, no psychology; it moves between the comic and the sad, and back again. I don't assume any right to judge my characters: like Jean Renoir, I think that everyone has his own reasons for behavior."

Our Generation

"Also I'm a great believer in improvisation. I work practically without a shooting-script; all I prepare is the dialogue. And when I have scenes too delicate to be shot in the usual way like Antoine's scene with the psychologist in *The 400 Blows*, I clear everybody out and lock myself in, alone with the actors and the cameraman. You can't put the best moments of a film down in a script."

Truffaut attaches no importance to the label *nouvelle vague*: almost every week brings the first film of a new director to the Champs Elysées and that is the important thing.

"Certainly there's a great deal of rubbish. But to make itself felt, our generation will have to combine quality with quantity. Among the films of directors who haven't yet established themselves, I could mention at least two that, in my opinion, are more important than anything we have been shown so far. *Breathless* by Jean-Luc Godard and *Paris Belongs to Us* by Jacques Rivette. No matter who's at work in the cinema, the problems of trade and techniques are of less importance than people say. Good writers ought to film their own novels, and not let them fall into the hands of some third party. Once and for all the bluff of technique has to be killed. It paralyzes original expression."

"It's the Universe of Simenon"

YVONNE BABY / 1964

"ONCE MORE, AGAIN, THE SUBJECT is the most commonplace in the world: him, her, the other," wrote François Truffaut, who explained his choice to us.

"My idea was to make a film about adultery, inspired by the character of Pierre Jaccoud, which we know from the reports of the trial."

YB: *Why Jaccoud?*

FT: He touched me very much, and I thought that through him one could show a man that is strong in social life but weak in love and who, at 44 years old, finds himself in a sharp dilemma and more and more involved. *The Soft Skin* is a portrait of this man (Jean Desailly). We must follow him and identify with him.

YB: *Who is he exactly?*

FT: A grand bourgeois, but with something childish about him, which gives the impression of innocence and extreme clumsiness in secrecy. The key of the film is perhaps that men who have an exciting profession think of it constantly, whereas women only think of love. Love is a woman's affair.

YB: *And you make films about love . . .*

FT: Yes. Other subjects don't interest me. Each case deserves a film, and I could shoot 25 times the same scenes with different characters.

From *Le Monde*, 22 May 1964. Reprinted by permission of Yvonne Baby.

Jules and Jim says that one could love two men at the same time. *The Soft Skin* says the opposite. *Jules and Jim* was an idealization of love in the sense where the privileged characters lived privileged moments. Here, it is the universe of Simenon, the most everyday universe there is.

The film could resemble a news item that everybody reads in the press. News items disturb and fascinate because we find in them a mixture of fiction and fact.

YB: *Why did you make Françoise Dorléac an air hostess?*

FT: I would have preferred a young girl—a love affair with a secretary the age of Linda Baud seemed to me too painful—I felt like filming a travel adventure, scenes in a plane—we never see planes in flight in the cinema. The rest was a series of accidents, advantages, a Brazilian company gave me their support.

The extreme accuracy of documentary detail

YB: *Advantages but also difficulties . . .*

FT: Of another sort, like avoiding the "sordid." To achieve this, I evoked the scenes between the two lovers in a dreamlike manner—which corresponds to the state of love—and the scenes of married life with an almost excessive violence capable of giving the commonplace a tragic dimension.

YB: *Like the end of the film?*

FT: Yes. It was inspired by other passionate news items. In any case, I felt with certainty that it was necessary to reach an extreme point in the machine in which he was trapped and that death was the end.

What counts here is the accuracy of the documentary details and a certain way to go deep to stay close to reality while avoiding the conventional.

I always react against the previous film. After this one, I'm making *Fahrenheit 451* from a novel by Ray Bradbury. It will be lyrical, in color and I ask, will it perhaps resemble *The Soft Skin* and *Jules and Jim*?

François Truffaut: Film-Struck Truant

LEE LANGLEY/1966

FRANÇOIS TRUFFAUT is making a film in England. At
thirty-three he is acknowledged one of the top directors in France—
some say in the world. Six films have won him 24 international awards.
At Pinewood, making *Fahrenheit 451* based on the book by Ray Bradbury,
he is a foreigner working (for the most part through an interpreter)
with a film unit largely ignorant of his reputation. This is partly his
own doing. "Ask everyone you interview whether they can whistle the
music from *Shoot the Piano Player*," he instructed his assistant. "If they
can, don't hire them." He has a horror of being surrounded by a little
band of the faithful, prefering to work with strangers provided they are
totally professional.

Fahrenheit 451 stars Julie Christie and Oscar Werner—who appeared
in Truffaut's *Jules and Jim*. This morning another of the cast, Cyril
Cusack, in sleek black uniform of close-fitting trousers and narrow tunic
is running through a scene of improvised action. (Truffaut occasionally
likes to improvise action on set words or leave the dialogue fairly free
but adhere to formal rehearsed action.) Hovering behind the camera
the director watches his man closely.

Truffaut is slender; pale skin stretched taut over fragile bones . . . he
has nervous hands and a jutting romantic profile. Strong silver threads
glitter almost theatrically in his short-cropped black hair. His anxious
eyes are betrayed by a gleeful, hopeful grin. He hunches into his dark
overcoat, small, vulnerable, a prematurely aged Peynet Lover. He looks
frozen stiff.

From the *Guardian* (Manchester), 19 March 1966. © Guardian News & Media Limited,
1966. Reprinted by permission.

"I have never really felt young," he says. Yet he agrees with Cocteau's dictum that an art which is inaccessible to the young will never be an art. Does this mean that while he himself feels old, he thinks of his work as youthful? "More than youthful at the moment," he says gently, "juvenile! We're acting like schoolchildren on this film: the actors, the unit, me. We play with the fire-engines, ring the alarm-bells."

It is his first film in English, his first in a studio, his first in color, but he has no revolutionary ideas about the use of color in the cinema. At the same time, it isn't altogether naturalistic either; "the effect is very clear, bright and simple, like children's toys."

Truffaut's world always has an element of childhood wonder in it (even when he explored the adulterous territory of *The Soft Skin*). His first film, *Les Mistons* (*The Mischief-Makers*), was an evocation of adolescence, and *The 400 Blows* a backward glance at his own bitter childhood. He came to films through parental neglect and juvenile delinquency. The cinema was his escape, his dream-world. He has had the good fortune to make a career of his fantasy. Vis-à-vis the real world he is curiously detached.

Fahrenheit 451 is moving slowly today: the cold deepens as the morning ages, and the arc-lamps are sought like heaters by the numbed crowd below them. A realistic-looking lamp-post, needed for a previous shot, is laboriously chipped out of the pavement and removed because it inter-feres with the next shot.

At 14, Truffaut was running a film society, stealing copper door-knobs and selling them in the flea-market to pay for cinema seats. Eventually he landed in reform school. His difficult childhood has left scars.

Not sure, not sure

"I surround my own two daughters with love; I don't believe a happy childhood is bad for an artist's development. No, let us say rather what could be dangerous to an artist is to have a childhood without problems. And even then, I'm not sure, not sure."

He was rescued from the reform school by a remarkable man, a humanitarian journalist, André Bazin, who informed the principal that "a child can't be sent to a reform school for loving the cinema too much, even if he got the taste for it by playing truant . . ." He and his wife took the boy into their home and virtually adopted him. One of Truffaut's sharpest regrets is that Bazin died before *The 400 Blows* (dedicated to him) was acclaimed at the 1959 Cannes Film Festival and Truffaut voted Best Director. It was the vindication of his trust in a film-struck boy.

Set in some future electronic age, *Fahrenheit 451* deals with a society where firemen no longer put out fires. Instead, as guardians of the common weal, instructed by omnipresent television referred to as "The Family," they track down intellectuals harboring the forbidden possession: books, the root of unhappiness. Fahrenheit 451 is the temperature at which paper bursts into flame.

The film is being made in England for Universal Pictures because French distributors felt it was too expensive, too complicated, too original. Just as they previously thought *Jules and Jim* too absurd and *The Soft Skin* banal.

Lunch-break for Truffaut means a hurried half hour at his desk. While we talk he chews doggedly on fast-cooling lamb chop and chips, followed for some reason by thick soup. He hasn't lost his enthusiasm for film-going. "Last night I went to see *Citizen Kane* again," he says eagerly, "at Tooting Bec . . . You know Tooting Bec?"

In his teens, Truffaut spent every spare hour in the cinema: until about five years ago he kept a scrupulous record of all the films he saw (more than two thousand), some of them seen ten or more times. "That's more than four thousand hours that I suppose I should have spent reading or studying," he comments unrepentantly.

Renoir once said that to make films you have to possess a strong personal philosophy. Truffaut who admires Renoir deeply, agrees but adds that he can't really say what his is. "That should emerge in one's films . . . that's why one makes them."

The directors who have most influenced Truffaut are Renoir, Rossellini, and Hitchcock—he has just written a book, *Conversations with Hitchcock*, with the intention of reinstating Hitchcock in critical eyes—particularly American critical eyes—as a director of genius. "I think he's very much underrated, dismissed as a technician. I don't think people, especially American critics, really know or appreciate him sufficiently. He is the complete filmmaker."

Rossellini, however, is certainly the man who has had the most direct influence on Truffaut's development. "Before I met Rossellini, I wanted to make films of course, but it seemed impossible. A dream. He made it all seem easy. He has a powerful gift for simplification. He told me, it isn't hard to write a screenplay, you only have to look at the reality around you. He told me you mustn't copy the Americans—because of course until then they had been my masters—you mustn't go in for flashbacks, gimmicky credit . . . instead, plainness, simplicity."

"*The 400 Blows* owes a great deal to Rossellini. I made it like a documentary and three years earlier I wouldn't have been able to do that. I'd have thought of the American cinema. I didn't even like the documentary form, he showed me that things must be close to life."

First as a teenage enthusiast, later as a passionate, often vitriolic critic of the cinema on *Arts* and *Cahiers du Cinéma*, Truffaut has always been deeply concerned with American cinema. He believes, unfashionably, that it was at its best in the big studio, Goldwyn days.

Response to independence

"I don't think Americans respond well to independent production. Where American cinema was at its most unjust was with men of genius like Stroheim, Sternberg, Welles . . . but with middling good cinema it was at its best: people like Dassin and Preminger made their finest films for the studios, not when they became their own masters."

To talk of the *Nouvelle Vague* today is pretty old hat. Established, respectable, it has taken its place in historical context.

"I think filmmakers will begin younger and younger . . . boys of thirteen and fourteen will make films. After all, it's getting cheaper all the time to make them. The next step is for artists from other fields to find their way to directing films: poets, artists, and theatre people like Jean Genet, Sartre, Beckett, François Billetdoux . . ."

A friend has described Truffaut as "a business man in the morning, an artist in the afternoon." All his films have actually made money, in spite of their initial difficulties. He broods and agrees there is an element of truth in the tag. "I like to amuse myself by playing the business man from time to time. I'm co-producer on most of my films, and I like to know what things cost. Sometimes I say that's too expensive, we'll do it differently, but I can't imagine myself doing anything except direct films."

"I know my faults: I get too easily discouraged, for instance. I'm not hard enough. If I sense resistance, or see that what I want is not altogether acceptable, I don't fight. I say all right, we'll try it another way. People close to me say I should insist on doing it my way, but you know, with about sixty people round you, waiting, it's hard to keep them hanging about while you argue . . ."

He finds working in England easy—"I've been lucky because while I can't speak English, I've taught everyone to understand French . . ." He likes the British studio, the technical expertise, the comfort. He doesn't realize that some of the willingness he encounters is a response to his charm and childlike energy. "I'm always working"—he is even writing a diary of the making of *Fahrenheit 451* for *Cahiers du Cinéma* while shooting the film—"if I have nothing to do, I read, mostly books about the cinema . . ." Does he ever read books that have nothing to do with the cinema? Oh, yes, he exclaims confidently . . . Like? Well . . . like Chaplin's memoirs . . . he chuckles wryly, "you're right. They do always have a connection with the cinema . . ."

He never takes a holiday, although he sometimes arranges to have a screenplay to write so that he can be with his wife (daughter of a leading French film producer) and two children on their holidays. He doesn't need holidays, renews himself through working.

Truffaut once said that he had about 30 films about love in his head and intended to make them all in the next 45 years. If someone proved to him, he added, that nine out of ten films made were about love, he would still say it wasn't too much.

"Yes, I still believe that," he affirms. "There are very few films I like outside films about love in one form or another. For instance, I thought *Bridge on the River Kwai* was a stupid story. You need a story like that now and then, of course, but if you gave it to ten directors you'd get ten *Bridge on the River Kwai*'s. It would always be the same film. But if you gave a love story to ten different directors you get ten really different films. Because each puts so much of himself into it. This great human motor is our only common denominator."

A Problem of Calculating the Dose between the Everyday and the Extraordinary

YVONNE BABY / 1966

FT: At the end of 1960, I had a conversation with Raoul Lévy, and because I was violently attacking science fiction works, he told me several stories of this genre, one of which was *Fahrenheit 451*. In the society described by Ray Bradbury—where it is forbidden to read and where the firemen burn books—there was a fundamental idea that gave me the desire to make a film.

I met the author in 1962 in New York. I had the rights to his book and I started to work on it with my scenarist, Jean-Louis Richard. But we were disappointed to find out that it was very difficult to get the project off the ground in France even with Jean-Paul Belmondo, who loved the script, in the role of Montag. I had to wait four years before having the financial possibility to make the film in England. Anyway, the place, was not important: one could shoot *Fahrenheit* in London as much as in Stockholm or Toronto.

YB: *What were the problems that this film posed for you?*
FT: Vis-à-vis the public, the film was a kind of bet. Because everything was so simple, and the plot very eccentric that it was necessary to render it plausible, believable without losing the fantasy. Basically, it was a question of a dose of the everyday and the extraordinary and, without stopping, it was necessary to pass from one to the other and to mix them up.

From *Le Monde*, 18 September 1966. Reprinted by permission of Yvonne Baby.

When the scenario presented difficulties of construction, we told ourselves, "This is a story of the Resistance. Montag (the fireman) is part of the Gestapo. Clarisse (the young woman) is in the underground." In this way, we looked for a way of progressing while avoiding the possibility that *Fahrenheit* could lend itself to a political end or resemble a left-wing American film. With Montag, I showed, for the first time, a "positive hero," but I didn't want either that he had the air of an American film hero.

Fahrenheit is against power in general in the sense that power, time and again, underestimates culture or it gives it an exaggerated importance in pretending to believe that a film, a play, a novel—for example *La Religieuse, The Screens, Marat-Sade*—could really be dangerous.

What I like very much in Bradbury's invention is having imagined a law—by virtue of which all books are forbidden—he imagined, at the same time, a means of circumventing it. This consisted of learning the books by heart which, for me, is a sublime ruse.

To compensate for the feeling of exile

YB: *Is there a rapport between* Fahrenheit *and your earlier films?*
FT: Montag (Oscar Werner) is reminiscent of Jean-Pierre Léaud, the adolescent of *The 400 Blows*. He is in his normal universe until suddenly something small disturbs him. From the moment that he takes a book home with him and starts to read, he is caught in the works. It happens that he skips going to the fire station like skipping school.

My main reaction from *The Soft Skin* was to give the two female roles to the same actress to finally kill the duality or the contrast between the brunette and the blonde, etc. These roles are not very spectacular; one avoids the disadvantage of having a star's performance, all the more that Julie Christie portrayed them with equal modesty, without any preference for one or the other.

This time I tried to be realistic in the script and dreamlike in the shooting in creating in each scene, even normal ones, an imbalance, a malaise, an instability of which Hitchcock is the master and of which he taught us the secret.

In my other films, it seems to me I was sometimes first concerned with the characters and then sometimes the story. For *Fahrenheit*, the priority was to pay attention systematically to the visual side. If, finally, the film resembles a dream, then all the better.

YB: *Did the fact that you wrote a diary of the making of the film for* Cahiers du cinéma *influence your work at all?*
FT: I tried to keep a journal of *Jules and Jim*, and perhaps I didn't manage because I shot it in France with French people. But in London, to compensate for the feeling of being an exile, every evening, in my hotel room, I recounted, in two pages, what had happened that day. I realized that it helped me a lot to understand my work and to see things that one usually sees much later, in particular while editing the film.

In the same way, previously, it was necessary for me each week in *Arts*, for which I was a critic, when the screenplay of the films helped me a little to learn the job of a screenwriter.

A book as an object

YB: *Haven't you wanted to make a film about books for some time?*
FT: Yes, and I was influenced by certain articles by the writer Roger Caillois in the *Nouvelle Revue Française* on books and reading. He said that books have a different value according to individuals. He spoke of people, mostly academics, who are interested in the contents, and other people, mostly autodidacts who consider a book as an object which carries with it memories and sentiments. The film risks touching those, of which I am one, for whom books have great sentimental value.

The books chosen for *Fahrenheit* don't constitute a preferential catalogue. In certain cases, we tried to provoke an emotion by a memory, such as showing a copy of the collection *Le livre de demain*, published by Artheme Fayard, with the engraved wood which was very popular, and for all French audiences evoke the postwar period. And if we waited a long time in a current of air in which we see almost all the pages of a Dali album, it is because he is the only great artist who declared himself in favor of all forms of censorship.

Truffaut's *Bride Wore Black*

SIGHT AND SOUND / 1 9 6 7

"PERSONALLY," SAYS TRUFFAUT, "I'm always scared of publicity, and I think there are a lot of films to which it has been positively harmful. A film is complete in itself. It has its own intrinsic mystery, which can hold out against the vast publicity of stills, but not against things like trailers and TV extracts. That way, the spectator's curiosity has been satisfied. He's seen how it's put together and got an idea of its style. So why should he bother to go out to see it? I've noticed that films like *Au Hasard, Balthazar*, and *Mouchette*, which had a lot of extracts shown on television, weren't very successful. Even advertisements can sometimes spoil a film. I remember with Orson Welles' *The Trial*, one kept waiting for the shot of the typewriters, or of Anthony Perkins standing in front of the huge door, and was rather disappointed when it came.

"I think a film ought not to have too much of an existence before it has actually been screened. That's why, when it came to my own *The Bride Wore Black*, from the William Irish novel, I gave the press what amounted to a bogus synopsis—deliberately a long way off the film, and actually sounding much more than an Antonioni subject. It's a revenge story. There's an accident, a misunderstanding, a gun that ought not to have been loaded; and a woman finds that she is a widow on her wedding day. One by one she visits the men who knew her husband: one woman (Jeanne Moreau) set off against a whole number of men (Claude Rich, Brialy, Michel Bouquet, Michel Lonsdale, Charles Denner, and Daniel Boulanger). Because the film was to be in English,

---

From *Sight and Sound*, Autumn 1967. Reprinted by permission of *Sight and Sound*.

Jean-Louis Richard and I devised a non-speaking part for Boulanger. And we haven't changed it; he still doesn't speak a word.

"The film isn't in the least psychological: it's more like a feminine version of *Tirez sur le Pianiste*. The link is that all these men illustrate different ways of reacting towards a very pure, absolutely chaste woman. And as you know, I've always enjoyed this experimental mix-up of American themes and French temperament.

"We were trying to find a new subject for Jeanne Moreau that would have nothing in common with *Jules et Jim*. No laughing or smiling; this time I asked her for an absolutely neutral face, that of a professional absorbed in her work. It was when I was talking to Jeanne at the time of *Mata-Hari* that I remembered the book, and three or four unforgettable scenes in it which I could still visualise very clearly. The rights had been acquired by Al Bartlett, the American who specialises in stock shots of aircraft carriers, but he couldn't set up the production. Not surprising, really, because the end of the book is impossible: we had to find our own surprise ending . . .

"William Irish is a pseudonym used by Cornell Woolrich, the writer they call 'the thriller king.' There have been at least 22 American films from his novels and short stories: Tourneur's *The Leopard Man* (from *Black Alibi*), Siodmak's *Phantom Lady*; Harold Clurman's *Deadline at Dawn* (Clifford Odets did the adaptation); Arthur Ripley's *The Chase*; Maxwell Shane's *Fear in the Night*, and so on. There's also *The Night Has a Thousand Eyes* (Woolrich wrote this under the name of George Hopley, another of his pseudonyms); and, perhaps more successfully in cinema terms, Tetzlaff's *The Window*. And, of course, Hitchcock's *Rear Window*. And now, I hope, *The Bride Wore Black*.

"Camerawork by Raoul Coutard; classical progression (three short flashbacks and a nice twist in the plot); but by using locations that aren't readily identifiable I've tried to create the effect of an imaginary landscape, without specifically saying this was what I was doing. There are some country house scenes, and as the weather was fine we shot them outside, on the lawn, with the characters sitting around on white garden chairs. I must say it looks very English.

"In fact, I'll be interested to see if the critics say all the things again that they always say about my films, no doubt because I break dramatic conventions and so on. 'A film where nothing happens; a pallid film . . . etc.'

It really startled me when they said it again about *Fahrenheit,* because this was full of incident."

"This film is absolutely not a portrait of a woman. Jeanne Moreau is the central character, but even at the end we still don't really know anything about her. In *Jules et Jim,* Jim was the character one knew least about; and both of them are vehicles for taking the audience from one character to another. Each of the men she meets gets only a quarter of an hour and confides his most intimate secrets to her. In three scenes, we're supposed to know all about them—which of course is wildly improbable. I really love the whole atmosphere of this sort of hazy story, these grown-up fairytales where the characters aren't really crooks but just a little on the mad side.

"Basically, the challenge is the same as with *Fahrenheit*: to find just the right kind of tone and dialogue to make a very farfetched story seem true and plausible. But it's also a reaction against *Fahrenheit,* because it gave me a lot more personal freedom: there's no heroic element in this story—quite the contrary. Another compensation for me: in *Fahrenheit* I had altogether fifty minutes without dialogue; in *The Bride* I have a lot of talk. Even if Jeanne hardly opens her mouth, the others are all very free with their confidences; and, as in *Tirez sur le Pianiste,* I've lifted whole sentences out of the novel. *Les Dames du Bois de Boulogne* has the finest dialogue of any film I know. I can't resist it, and in all my films there are sentences from *Les Dames*—commonplace but stylised expressions, like *'surtout ne me remerciez pas.'*

"Organising a picture is rather like shuffling cards, preventing the spectator from sympathising with one character rather than another. The whole job of shooting is a matter of balance, weighing the scales so that no one's caught at a disadvantage. It's the exact opposite of the Audiard-Gabin style, where Gabin is always allowed the last word, the hero's gesture, even if he hasn't opened his mouth right through the scene. But whenever I feel the audience may be making up their minds about a character, I always try to switch their sympathies around . . .

"A lot of films are harmed by cutting. *La Peau Douce* would originally have run for 135 minutes, and 25 minutes cut from the original script did it no good. So I try not to shoot anything I'm not going to use, to keep a careful time check, and to pick up time somewhere else if it looks as though we are over-running on length.

"When I've just finished a script, I always feel that it's very accessible: clear, neat, and well-scrubbed. If there's anything subversive it comes out only when you start shooting. Suddenly, I find that I no longer want to make something that people are going wholly to believe in. In forty films, after all, Renoir has never been able to bring himself to create a wholly odious character: even Dalban, in *Toni*, had charm. When you're shooting, you find yourself saying: 'I don't want to fool the public; I want them to understand that all I'm doing is shooting a film . . .'

"Godard is inimitable in this, as in everything else. His films are more and more like personal confidences. If his audience has dwindled a bit lately, it's because films live off a larger public than the one for which they are designed. And all that's happened with Godard is that now his films are finding their real audience: the people who are the ones who enjoy what he's doing. He really is the first film-maker for addicts. He has found a way of conquering the two or three worst things I know about the audience: polite indifference, vague interest, amused condescension. He has pulverised the system, and turned the cinema upside down, just as Picasso did with painting; and like Picasso, he's made everything possible. Finally, he's got away from the mystique of scarcity value. Before Godard, people who made a lot of films were commercial hacks. Since he took to making almost three pictures a year, a lot of other people have adjusted their ideas about speed. The number of important films is growing; there's no longer that lengthy pause while we wait for the big director to come up with another one."

The Cinema according to Truffaut

PETER LENNON/1967

BY NOW THE MAIN POINTS of François Truffaut's career are fairly generally known: he was the pugnacious young critic on *Arts* and the *Cahiers du Cinéma* who helped to lead the attack on the entrenched film industry of the fifties, and went on to demonstrate that not only could he tell people what was wrong with their films but he could do better himself.

His *The 400 Blows* won both the Grand Prix and the International Catholic Office Award at the Cannes Festival of 1959. This and Resnais's *Hiroshima Mon Amour* were the beginning of the "new wave" which was to make the hand-held camera, improvisation, and a low budget characteristic of the young French cinema.

A zany adaptation of the American thriller *Shoot the Piano Player*, a year later and *Jules and Jim*, in which Jeanne Moreau dropped her morose mask and went all gay, solidly established Truffaut as one of the really high-class talents in the French cinema. *The Soft Skin* (1963) was less satisfactory and *Fahrenheit 451* last year made some glum. Now, with Moreau again, he has begun shooting at Cannes, an adaptation of another American thriller, *The Bride Wore Black*. Is it going to be another brilliant and personal *Shoot the Piano Player* or a piece of imitation Americana?

Not like Godard

Truffaut is a very classical director. His set is quite unlike a Godard set, where the actors are given their lines on dirty little scraps of paper, like food tickets: a thin scatter of technicians stand around looking as if they were waiting for the real crew to turn up; and the director potters about finding this bit on to that while everyone wonders what the film is about.

At Cannes, working in wide screen and color, while still very far from the technical inferno of a big MGM production, it was the familiar large crowd of actors and technicians working more or less strictly to a detailed script. Truffaut is very painstaking—a minimum of seven takes for each shot—and meticulous: Claude Rich giving his friend Jean-Claude Brialy the high sign to be left alone with Jeanne Moreau had to "straighten the eyebrows . . . No, not the lips. The eyes just a little to the left. No, not too much . . . keep the forehead smooth: the head steady . . ." We got a creak in the neck watching.

It was a cocktail party high in a sunny residence overlooking the bay at Cannes. The mysterious Moreau is being enigmatic and provocative with her hosts: Rich and Jean-Claude Brialy. Laconic dialogue; search-ing looks: a waiter with a tray; the tense move to the balcony . . . some-thing terrible is going to happen! On the surface it was ticking over very much à la Hitchcock.

Personally, at 35, Truffaut still retains some of the air of his tough teenage life in the streets of Paris. A kind of John Garfieldian figure: tense, rapid in his speech, restless, and unquiet; in his attitudes very human and concerned. He is frank to the point of being unguarded and indiscreet.

He is indiscreet about other directors—"I wouldn't go to see *Ulysses*"—and unguarded about his own difficulties. He admits that in *The Soft Skin* it was a mistake to stick rigidly to the news item which inspired the film: a betrayed wife walked into a restaurant in the Latin Quarter and blasted her husband with a shot-gun. It was an unconvinc-ingly violent end for a film which had sensitively described the weari-ness and the lugubrious aspects of an illicit affair.

He does not feel that *Fahrenheit 451* was a failure, but he admits that shooting in English was a mistake. For one thing Oscar Werner got out of hand. "In *Jules and Jim* I knew French, but he didn't. But in *Fahrenheit* I didn't know English but he did. I prefer it the other way," he said with a wry smile.

"Actors? The problem with Werner was that he, the stage actor, came to the part with a ready-made idea which was not at all mine.

Originally I wanted James Mason. Jeanne Moreau, on the other hand, is perfect. She never goes to rushes, hardly reads the script, she is completely 'available.' She has to be rigorously directed, but she brings a lot of authority to a part.

Actors' freedom

"Yes, sometimes I will let an actor improvise. When Jean-Pierre Léaud talked to the police psychiatrist in *The 400 Blows* I let him tell his own anecdote. I had imagined the part a little more gloomy, but I took some of Léaud's gaiety and flourishing youthful quality. In *The Soft Skin*, I let Françoise Dorleac reminisce also. It depends very much on the actor."

"The reason I shoot a scene so many times is that I'm bringing the actor imperceptibly from the rehearsal stage to the actual performance. I don't like the style: Now everyone ready, we are going to do it seriously . . ."

Why does he make thrillers? "Because we can't make Westerns. The Western, the musical comedy, the sophisticated thriller are the Americans'. We are left with thrillers. In *Shoot the Piano Player* I was paying my debt to the American cinema. It was not a farce, or a parody like *Cat Ballou*—a respectful pastiche, if you like . . ."

"I think that you have everything in a director's first film," he said. "He can be better or worse later, but it's all in the first film. *Citizen Kane*, for example. For myself you have it all in my first short *Les Mistons (The Mischief-Makers)*, which was made in 1958."

Social problems? "There is nothing social in my films. No, there were no social implications in the prison scenes in *The 400 Blows*. I am completely asocial. I never vote and I don't have a library card. Because I don't think voting serves any purpose. Nobody wanted De Gaulle in 1958 and he got in. There was a general strike to prevent him getting full powers recently and he got them. Even if there was social criticism in the Bradbury book there is none in my film.

"I think I'm closest to Demy—*The Umbrellas of Cherbourg*—in his aspect of playing a game. Making films is an escape from reality."

Which brought us to the tricky subject: how did he account for the fact that French film critics read such bizarre meanings into so many third-rate Hollywood films. Their recent reading of Raoul Walsh's old B weepy *The Man I Love* was a good example.

Truffaut gives a perfect example of it himself in his recently published book on Hitchcock, made up of 50 hours of interviews, *The Cinema According to Hitchcock.*

Speaking of an incident in *North by Northwest* Truffaut says: "You have the religion of gratuitousness, the taste for fantasy founded in the absurd." And the crafty old Cockney replies smoothly: "The fact is I practice this taste for the absurd absolutely religiously."

The absurdities

What were they talking about? A farmer getting on a bus which is about to drive off and leave Cary Grant stranded on a lonely road says: "That's funny. That plane is spraying crops and there ain't no crops to spray." Metaphysical absurdity? Or is the audience simply being given a hint that this is no innocent plane but one out to get Cary Grant. Ask any schoolboy!

Would the explanation be that French critics are weak on English? Truffaut looked as vague as an extremely alert, quick-witted, and experienced director can manage to look. "Maybe . . . In any event," he said. "I always preferred the dubbed versions. I used to learn the dialogue off by heart."

The Bride Wore Black Is a Film of Pure Sentiment

YVONNE BABY/1968

"I READ THE WILLIAM IRISH NOVEL at the Liberation," Truffaut tells us. "I was about 13. I read a little in secret when I was alone in the house, because my mother had told me it was terrifying. In 1964, I spoke about it to Jeanne Moreau and, by one of those accidents in life when one finds something old at the precise moment when one thinks of it, the novel, whose title I had forgotten, was republished meanwhile by *Club du livre policier*.

"I therefore doubted whether it was the same book. I re-read it and the reading encouraged me to make the film: a love story entirely linked to the events preceding the narration, and which allowed me to make another film with Jeanne Moreau but not to have any scene which could resemble any in *Jules and Jim*. I wanted to work with Jeanne Moreau again after *Jules and Jim*, but not that kind of story."

YB: *Is there any similarity between* The Bride Wore Black *and your precedent film,* Fahrenheit 451?
FT: *The Bride* is very close to *Fahrenheit* by its dreamlike atmosphere, its familiar science fiction aspect, but different from it in the manner where, this time, I'm not treating a "big subject." *Fahrenheit*, which was basically a "film-object," could have given the impression of having, for example, the theme of "the respect for literature." This theme was, of course, implicit. I never thought of *Fahrenheit* as a thesis or message film.

From *Le Monde*, 18 April 1968. Reprinted by permission of Yvonne Baby.

YB: *And this one?*

FT: It pretends to tell a romantic story like in the cinema of recent years. Julie Kohler (the "bride") became a widow on her wedding day. Her husband, in fact, collapses beside her as they come out of the church, and she decides to find, one by one, those who were responsible for the murder. She absolutely doesn't envisage remaking her life. She thinks of only one mission: to avenge her husband.

Her enquiry leads her to meet, in different places, five men who were involved, either to woo them or to make them confess to her. And each episode reflects their attitude towards women.

The great advantage was that I used a police adventure plot. If the story is very simple and if the situations are very clear, I can use dialogue in a way that is completely independent of the story. This works alone, and we get two parallel films that progress simultaneously.

YB: *Is it that which creates the sensation of a dream?*

FT: Perhaps. This sensation is already felt in the mad writing in the novels of William Irish, who was the kind of writer in the collection entitled *Serie Rose* concurrent, in a certain epoch, with the *Serie Noire*. Compared with the literature of brutality and violence, his was a literature of nightmare and forbidden love.

YB: *So you have made another film about love . . .*

FT: Yes. I think it's the best subject. I have an idea that if you suggest to two directors to make *The Bridge on the River Kwai*, they'll both make the same film. But if you suggest to them the subject of *Brief Encounter*, they will certainly make a different film. To speak of love requires a greater gift and obliges one to go beyond the frame of just telling a story.

The Bride is actually a love film but of pure sentiment because it concerns a past love for Julie. On the screen, she is a sort of living dead. She only survives to avenge her husband.

Around her, the men are representative of different types, the timid, the audacious, the collectors of women, or the romantics. They appear to Julie in relation to the absolute which David, her husband of five minutes, embodied.

For them, Julie is not normal and, every one of them, in turn, dreams of more or less entering her life.

There is always the question of ethics

YB: *Is there a link between her and other women characters in your films?*
FT: As usual, it's the women who take the initiative, and who, without losing any of her femininity, manipulates men having their vulnerability in common. Here, Julie's mission, in our eyes, inhuman and extravagant, is for her merely work to be accomplished. And it is not difficult to imagine that there is nothing more for her to do once the task is completed.

It is in contrast to Catherine in *Jules and Jim* whose life is full of sexual liberty. Julie is, without any doubt, still a virgin. But the two heroines come together in their moral intransigence, because, here or there, it is always a question of ethics even if I have more and more the taste for disguising it in film divertissements. One mustn't conceal that such an enterprise constitutes a game; a game of the director with his film; a game of the film with the public.

The Bride can seem simplistic and mechanical to whoever refuses to admit that an adult film can begin with "Once upon a time. . . ." For me and also for my actors, *The Bride* is nevertheless a serious film. Because one cannot film death for 56 days without being affected. Besides, I am convinced that the first scene of death shot by a director marks a stage in his career. This hit me when I moved from *The 400 Blows* to *Shoot the Piano Player*, in which I was already forced voluntarily to film material very far from my own personal experience. That of American novels that I love so much and among which *The Bride* is a classic.

I would like to say finally that the five men that Julie finds in her path brings us back to the principal of enumeration which makes fairy tales so fascinating: *Goldilocks and the Three Bears, The Three Little Pigs and the Wicked Wolf, Snow White and the Seven Dwarfs . . .*

YB: *How do you evoke this fairy tale atmosphere?*
FT: By a constant effort of simplification and visual stylization. For example, at the end of the only scene which unites the five men, the script says: "They decide to separate and never try to see each other again." And the image shows, disregarding any credibility, the five friends descending a fire escape and who, on arriving at the bottom, leave in all different directions.

On the other hand, in a film in color, Julie is dressed only in black and white, and, rather than entering a scene and leaving it, one could say that she appears and disappears. This dream-like character is considerably reinforced by Bernard Hermann's score (the composer of Welles' *Citizen Kane* and Hitchcock's *Vertigo*) which draws the film towards opera. That suits me because it's another mask.

Like a skilled worker

YB: *You quote Hitchcock and you admire him. Has this film been influenced by him?*
FT: Certainly, for the construction of the plot, because, unlike the novel, we give the solution to the enigma well before the end of the film. So the public don't have to wait long for an explanation which, even though ingenious, rarely deserves to constitute the end of a film.

On the other hand, the wish to get the characters to talk about something else other than the plot is not very Hitchcockian but more characteristic of a European way of thinking. Between Renoir and Hitchcock, I have always thought that Cocteau made a point. A long time before *The Bride*, didn't he speak of "filming Death at work"?

There are six violent deaths in *The Bride* and one can for this reason believe that it's a film of situations. It's probably to struggle against this danger that I paid particular attention to the characters. And I chose before writing the adaptation and the dialogue with my friend Jean-Louis Richard, the six actors who would accompany Jeanne Moreau: Claude Rich and Jean-Claude Brialy, who I see as Pinter characters; Michel Bouquet who reminds me perhaps of Audiberti for those who know him; Michel Lonsdale, a dilettante politician like Jean Dutourd; Daniel Boulanger whose body is so expressive that it was not necessary to give him one word to speak, and Charles Denner, whose career was launched with *Landru*, who proved that a collector of women, from one day to another, will bring himself to say, "I love you."

As for Jeanne Moreau, it was necessary for her role of illusion. Nothing is more satisfactory for an audience than a character that goes as far as she can. And for this journey in a straight line, we agreed with her that it should be played without artifice, without coquetry and seriously and lightly at the same time. I hope that Jeanne Moreau in *The Bride* make one think less of a goddess of vengeance than an obstinate and competent person. I asked her to play it like a skilled worker.

The 400 Blows of François Truffaut

GILLES JACOB / 1968

FOR THE LAST FEW MONTHS, the French cinema has been in a state of uproar. In May, the Cannes Festival was brought to an abrupt halt; and at the same time in Paris the *Etats Généraux du Cinéma* came into existence, full of reformist optimism and doomed to failure. More recently, a directors' co-operative has been started; but film-makers have such divergent interests, and the differences between them are so wide, that it's hard to see exactly who or what this organization is likely to benefit.

In Philippe Labro's new book *Ce n'est qu'un Début*, François Truffaut outlines the circumstances which led (with a little help from him) to the shut-down of Cannes. People have argued that it wasn't for him to intervene, that neither he nor his friends were Jury members, that they hadn't been invited to show their films in or out of competition, in fact that the Festival was not theirs to close. Now they can read his expressions of regret—perhaps rather belated—at having had to send foreign visitors packing, clutching their cans of film under their arms, inadequately informed about what was going on, and in general perplexed by their peculiar welcome.

But in the light of recent events, it seemed to me interesting to try to follow up Truffaut's own attitude. Fiercely individualistic, and hitherto thought of as asocial, he has twice gone into battle alongside film-makers more revolutionary than himself—as fervently militant supporter of Henri Langlois during the Cinémathèque crisis, and as one of those who brought Cannes to a grinding halt. At the same time, he

From *Sight and Sound*, Autumn 1968. Reprinted by permission of *Sight and Sound*.

decided to take no part in the work of the *Etats Généraux du Cinéma*, and has not joined the new film-makers' co-operative. His position could look inconsistent: he runs the risk of antagonizing both those who regarded him as a reasonable man and those who did not. It's this position which Truffaut defends and develops in the following interview.—G.J.

GJ: *Why did you stop the Cannes Festival?*
FT: Because it was the *logical* thing to do. France was closing down, therefore Cannes had to close down. While I was driving to Cannes on May 17 to take part in a press conference about the Cinémathèque affair, I was listening to the radio and every half-hour came reports of more factories being occupied. I wasn't sorry to see France paralyzed, the government in disarray. Next day, when I asked for the Festival to be stopped, I wasn't thinking particularly of a gesture of solidarity with the workers—I'd have been more likely to feel solidarity with the four students who were sentenced to jail after a hasty session in a Sunday court. I wasn't really thinking of challenging or reforming the Festival, of doing away with evening dress or making it more cultural. No, I just felt that in its own interest the Festival should stop of its own accord rather than be halted a few days later by the force of events. I didn't see it as a military coup, I simply wanted an unambiguous situation. In fact, this is how it happened.

During the night, I was told of the creation of the *Etats Généraux du Cinéma* and their decision to stop the Festival, and I talked to a few people about it. We had no idea how difficult it is to stop this kind of big business event. We just adopted the tactics that had worked for the Cinémathèque: producers who had films in competition would withdraw them, jury members would resign. We made a mistake in not giving more information about the situation in France to people who for a week had been reading nothing but the Festival daily. (You feel differently according to whether or not you've been listening to the news.) This was especially true of foreign journalists and delegates, who naturally had qualms about joining in an anti-government movement . . .

Anyway, we had to get the Festival stopped and we did. It could maybe have been managed more elegantly, but in circumstances like this you're inclined to check your manners with your hat—and someone probably throws away the cloakroom key. I know that a lot of people will hold our attitude at Cannes against us for a long time to come, but I also know that a few days later, when there were no more planes and no more trains, when the telephones weren't working and we'd run out of petrol and cigarettes, the Festival would have looked utterly ridiculous if it had tried to carry on.

GJ: *Did you sign any manifestos in support of the student movement?*
FT: I'm not a professional campaigner. For four months, I'd devoted all my energies to the Cinémathèque affair, in the hope that it could be resolved. The Government was in the wrong over the *Affaire Langlois—* this is basic, everyone recognizes it—and it backed down because people weren't just protesting but protesting in the streets. In February, in the Place du Trocadéro, one of Malraux's decisions was really challenged for the first time. I am not politically-minded and as a rule I try to steer clear of this kind of thing, but after what happened in February I wanted to see the end of this regime.

GJ: *Can you remind us what stand you took in the Cinémathèque affair?*
FT: The Cinémathèque is a private association of 780 members who are also film depositors. The films they deposit make up a considerable part of the Cinémathèque's treasure. In return for the subsidy it allocated annually, the Government had acquired a majority on the Administrative Council. You may say that Langlois and his friends were wrong to let this situation develop. My answer is that Langlois, who might have been suspicious of any ordinary Minister, put his trust in Malraux. In the beginning, everyone trusted Malraux . . . Anyway, when on February 9 the Government took over the Cinémathèque, without first consulting members of the Association, it was using tactics that it has used else-where: subvention, then a controlling hand, then absorption. If an organization doesn't "think" the same way as the Government, there's a real risk that it may find itself losing its subsidy . . .

GJ: *In effect, the Cinémathèque affair gave you something in common with the students. What was it that drew you to the Latin Quarter during the trou-bles?*
FT: The really admirable thing about the student movement, I think, is that it's not self-interested. In May and June I didn't want to go to the

Sorbonne. It was too much the smart thing to do, and wrong because it was their affair and their home ground. But I did go quite a lot to the Odéon. It was often very fine. You felt the need of a place where anyone can say anything he likes, as they have in the streets, in London.

GJ: *While you weren't afraid to stop the enormous machinery of the Cannes Festival, you've refrained from collaborating in any of the reform projects of the* Etats Généraux du Cinéma, *either on its special committees or in the General Assembly. Why?*

FT: I didn't want to join in the *Etats Généraux du Cinéma,* because I felt that 1,200 people from the profession, meeting together at Suresnes, would never manage to agree. There were workers there who wanted a production output of 140 films a year instead of 80; and now that TV keeps so many of the public in their homes that just isn't possible. There were artists who wanted more freedom and consequently fewer Union restrictions . . . but without the Unions actually losing anything. And of course there were would-be directors who had little hope of getting into the profession and were looking for a revolution and a brand new start from scratch. All these meetings and projects were really doomed to failure. I might add that they would have been doomed even if we had a left-wing government, because no government of any sort is likely to put the affairs of the cinema high among its priorities.

GJ: *Are you a member of the New Directors' Association?*

FT: After the failure of the *Etats Généraux* became obvious, two new technicians' unions were created, as well as a filmmakers' association presided over by Robert Bresson and Robert Enrico, with Albicocco, Louis Malle, Doniol-Valcroze among its more active members. I believe they have already collected about a hundred names, but I still don't want to join them. Why not? Perhaps because I don't have much collective or even comradely spirit. I feel solidarity with Rivette or Godard or Rohmer because I like them and admire their films, but I don't feel I have much in common with Jacqueline Audry or Serge Bourguignon, or Jacques Poitrenaud. The fact that we are all working at the same profession doesn't mean a thing to me, unless friendship and respect are also involved.

I dislike approaching problems in terms of generalities. It really infuriated me, for instance, to see all the projects of the *Etats Généraux* beginning with attacks on the existing production system because of the "profit motive." Films like *Hiroshima mon Amour* or *Pierrot le Fou* were produced and distributed with courage and discernment. In some East European countries they would have been locked up in a cupboard for a couple of years before the authorities hesitantly let them out; and in Hollywood someone would have come along and re-edited them. The European system seems the best to me simply because it isn't really a system.

GJ: *To sum up: you're not opposed to film-makers operating from commercial motives, and if you did stop the show at Cannes it wasn't necessarily for the same reasons as some of your fellow-directors.*

FT: I personally would rather work for a producer who gives me a hundred million francs because he expects to get back a hundred and thirty million, than have to submit a script to a State committee which will authorize a subsidy after it approves the contents. I'll go so far as to say that, concession for concession, it seems to me less shaming to have to give a film a happy ending for commercial reasons than to have to shoot an optimistic ending for ideological reasons. Anyway today, on July 20, the anniversary of the unsuccessful attempt on Hitler's life, I think that all films should end with the mushroom cloud over Hiroshima. Because that's what is in store for us, don't you think?

Life Style of Homo Cinematicus

SANCHE DE GRAMONT/1969

A LITTLE GIRL WAS TAKEN to see a movie on the life of
Joan of Arc. When she got home her mother asked what it was about
and she said, "It's about a lady who is burned at the stake and then
becomes a shepherd girl." This could only be a François Truffaut story,
because it explores the way movies improve on life—continuous performance cancels the sequence of events.

Aside from being a much-admired film director, Truffaut is a charter
member of a new species, the "homo cinematicus," who is concerned—
to the exclusion of nearly all other pursuits—with life at 24 frames a
second. When a long-lost friend ran into him recently and asked,
"What has happened to you in the last 10 years?" he replied, "I made
nine films." When he is not making films he is watching them (he has
seen *Citizen Kane* 27 times), so that much of what he sees around him
reminds him of old movies. He sees a poster in a metro station and
says, "That's like the poster in Renoir's *Le Crime de M. Lange*." In a cafe
he says, "That bartender looks like the bartender in *High Noon*." He
overhears a snatch of street conversation and it reminds him of the dialogue in an old Jean Gabin movie.

He prefers Nice for holidays because it is the only vacation spot in
France with 40 movie houses. He is embarrassed when life intrudes on
his screen memories. One evening he was eating alone in a Paris restaurant when Marlene Dietrich made an entrance with a gossip columnist
who waved at Truffaut as they passed his table. "Is that François

From the *New York Times Magazine*, 15 June 1969. Reprinted by permission of Sanche de
Gramont.

Truffaut?" asked Marlene. "Oh, but I adored *The 400 Blows* and *Jules and Jim*. I must meet him, do bring him over." The columnist leapt to Truffaut's table to deliver the message. Truffaut blushed, shook his head, and said, "No, no, no, no, no." "But just the other day you were telling me how you adored *The Scarlet Empress*—von Sternberg, Marlene married on horseback, her shimmering veil . . ." "I can't," said Truffaut, "I admire her too much," and he put his nose on his plate.

Even Truffaut's biography is revealed through blessed celluloid. The opening scene of *Stolen Kisses* shows his recurring nonhero, Antoine Doinel, being released from a military prison and given a dishonorable discharge. Cutting back to Truffaut at age 20, we see him smoking cotton-and-aspirin cigarettes to get classified 4F, but then, inexplicably, enlisting in the Foreign Legion, deserting just before his unit is due to leave for Indochina, tuning himself in, jailed, and discharged thanks to the influence of friends.

But many of Truffaut's biographical allusions can only be understood by his close relatives. Who else can guess that Antoine's girl friend carries a violin case because Truffaut's aunt used to carry one in the afternoon on the way to the Paris Conservatory? Sometimes the autobiographical reference is transposed. In *The 400 Blows*, Antoine tells the school principal, to explain his absences, that his mother has died. What Truffaut actually told a teacher during the Occupation was that his father had been arrested by the Germans.

Other sections of *The 400 Blows* are lifted directly from Truffaut's own experience. Like Antoine, François was always in trouble with school authorities, and his father was summoned by a juvenile court judge and told him: "Just think, your honor, he hates sports, he prefers to ruin his eyesight in movie houses." He forged so many sick notes that the principal called in his mother and told her: "We can't keep your son any longer, madame, his health is too frail." Truffaut ran away from home, sleeping in subway stations and at the houses of friends whose parents were away, and after two weeks he was caught and sent to a juvenile-delinquent center. Like the teenager in *The 400 Blows*, his head was shaved.

Aside from being the most autobiographical of the New Wave directors, Truffaut has retained from his rebellious youth an indelible suspicion of authority. He has never voted or adopted a political position because he is unable to think of himself as a citizen. When he received an embossed invitation from General de Gaulle for the annual arts-and-letters parties, at which the French artistic and intellectual community lines up in single file at the Elysee to hear a few words of encouragement from the chief of state (to a comedian: "Monsieur, you have often made me laugh"), he sent the invitation back. He remembered the time when he was 14 and was arrested for stealing a typewriter, and two policemen came into his cell and said, "Why don't you admit you masturbate at night and we'll leave you in peace?" He remembered the director of his summer camp during the Occupation who sold food and supplies to the Germans. Life remains for him a conflict between children and adults, between those in control of society and those on its margins.

He stands back, quizzical and mistrustful, from all issues. When he was asked to sign an anti-Vietnam-war manifesto, he said, "I refuse to condemn the Americans like that, with a signature. There is no such thing as wolves and sheep, there are wolves on both sides . . . A country at war which has the atom bomb and does not use it is giving a present to the other side."

Only once has he committed himself to a public issue, and that, predictably enough, involved movies. In 1968, some bureaucrats at the Ministry of Culture tried to oust Henri Langlois as director of the Government-subsidized Cinematheque, the world's outstanding film library. Langlois was the spiritual father of the New Wave directors. Truffaut, revealing an unsuspected gift for polemical efficiency, campaigned for months on his behalf by securing pledges from important directors that they would withdraw their films from the Cinematheque unless Langlois was reinstated. The opening shot of *Stolen Kisses* shows the locked gates of the Palais de Chaillot Cinematheque, the closing of which was as shocking to Truffaut as torture in Algeria had been to Jean-Paul Sartre. Thanks largely to Truffaut's efforts, Langlois got his job back and the Cinematheque reopened.

In order to grasp what the Cinematheque meant to Truffaut, let us listen to Henri Langlois as he sprawls on the banquette of a cafe like a large aquatic mammal, sipping warm grape juice and dispensing the cinematic gospel: "The New Wave generation (primarily Truffaut, Godard, Claude Chabrol, Louis Malle, and Alain Resnais) was weaned in the Cinematheque; they learned to observe life by watching films. King Vidor never used a shooting script, and these young directors worked from the direct observation of life. They were not professionals; most of them had never worked as assistant directors; they had never been taught what not to do. It was the triumph of antiprofessionalism.

"They showed there was no conflict between artistic and commercial success—*The 400 Blows* was voted the best foreign film of 1959 in the U.S. They restored dignity to their profession, whereas in America after Black Friday, Hollywood became cautious, barred the road to genius and relied on formulas. These young directors, so different in their sensibilities, formed a school in the same sense as the Impressionists did, in that they were against academic values and were able to express themselves freely.

"Take Truffaut. He is classic and not afraid to be. He is the complete opposite of the 'I want to be new and brilliant' school, but his films are like faces that will never show wrinkles. Like Renoir and Chaplin, he is his own rival, he is in that category of directors who are compared to themselves."

After his beginnings as a juvenile delinquent and a Foreign Legion deserter, Truffaut continued his misspent life as a movie critic. He laid down the law in the *Cahiers du Cinema* like a Spanish inquisitor, condemning directors of bad movies to prison and worse, and roasting the "Oscar collectors" as mere hacks, who, according to commercial requirements, went from a Bible spectacular to a western to a comedy on divorce with no urge to present their own vision of life. Truffaut's articles caused him to be banned from the Cannes Film Festival, but after *The 400 Blows* he returned as a member of the jury in 1960, the only decision he regrets. "The prizes were awarded frivolously," he recalls. "There were 11 judges, each with different interests, there were pressures, compromises, unexplained changes of mind, and we finally agreed on a film no one was against."

Along with his tastes and associations, Truffaut's personal life became subordinated to films. He never considered marrying outside the industry, and was hesitating between Hitchcock's daughter Patricia and one of Renoir's nieces when he met the daughter of a French producer named Morgenstern. The knot was soon tied, and she brought as her dowry the $80,000 loan Truffaut needed to make *The 400 Blows*. He established his own production company, which he called Coach Films in honor of Jean Renoir's *The Golden Coach*. He now has two daughters, 8 and 10, whom he is training to be script-girls. He has always kept complete control over his films, from the choice of subject and actors to the final cut.

The private Truffaut is revealed inferentially through his attitude toward his work. His shyness is reflected in the kind of people he chooses to work with, like assistant director Jean-José Richer and script-girl Suzanne Schiffmann. They must be reserved and natural; he cannot bear loud, pushy types. He uses the formal *"vous"* form of address with everyone—a way of discouraging familiarity—and he remembers as an important event in his life the time when he was working as Roberto Rossellini's assistant and announced that he was getting married, and Rossellini said, "In that case we must now say *tu* to one another." In most of his films there is a reference to the *tu-vous* dialectic, as when Charles Aznavour in *Shoot the Piano Player* tells a gangster, "I forbid you to use the *tu* form when addressing me," and the gangster repeats the dialogue using *vous*.

Truffaut is incurably French, and does not travel well. Once he went to Rome to make a picture for Dino de Laurentiis, starring Princess Soraya. When he arrived, he drank an iced tomato juice which upset his stomach. "I got panicky and thought, 'I don't want to die in Rome,' and I took the next flight back to Paris," he says. When he was in London shooting *Fahrenheit 451*, he felt no rapport with the English crew, since he speaks only French. Off the set he holed up in the London Hilton for six months, and had his meals brought to his room. When he got back to Paris, his friends asked him what swinging London was like. "I don't know," he said. "I just got out of the Hilton."

When he is on his home ground, however, there is a remarkably relaxed and friendly atmosphere on the set, as there was when I attended a postsynchronization session of *Mississippi Mermaid*, with Catherine Deneuve and Jean-Paul Belmondo, the French star-equivalents of Burton and Taylor, except that they only have to see each other during working hours. Truffaut, a little wiry man with melancholy black eyes, was in shirtsleeves, smoking a Gauloise, and might easily have been mistaken for the assistant grip, the one who is sent out for coffee and fixes the plumbing in the star's trailer. He walks on his heels like Charlie Chaplin, with quick, short steps, and he speaks to actors as though he feared he was intruding. He uses the method developed by Maria Montessori with small children—"Never raise your voice with an actor," he says.

I had been warned that Deneuve is like a barometer on a set; when she is not pleased with the film she is stormy. She tends to be hypercritical, to sit in judgment, but here she was radiant, unapproachably beautiful and yet joking with the technicians. She was the girl who walks into a room to have every man present fall in love with her on the spot. One of the script-girls, a drab, average woman, had a scarf tied to her waist, and Deneuve asked, "Is that so you won't forget something?" and the script-girl said, "It's so I won't forget I exist." The barometer was set at sunny and fair. I later saw a rumor published in *Paris Match* that the good feelings between her and Truffaut were more than professional. Belmondo stopped sparring with a technician long enough to say that "Truffaut's great with actors. He's like a good fight manager; he only talks to you when it's important."

Most actors are singularly inarticulate when they are not speaking someone else's lines, however, and it remained for Truffaut himself to explain the mechanisms of his art in the following monologue, which is exactly the kind of long statement he avoids in his own films, calling them "tunnels":

"Before I made any, I was drawn to very different kinds of films, and I never asked myself what kind of picture I would make. But when I started I decided on children, because I had to talk about what I knew, and outside of movies I knew nothing.

"I had suffered because I was an only child and I felt I was still close to the world of children; so I make *The 400 Blows* almost like a documentary. I was no martyr, but my parents left me alone a lot (my father was an industrial designer and my mother was a secretary), and they often went to the movies; so when they went away weekends I would go see the movies they had been talking about. I did odd things. When Paris was liberated I waited for G.I.'s to come out of the Pigalle subway station to show them the whorehouses so I'd have a little chewing gum.

"And then I had so many examples of disorderly lives around me that I told myself—and I haven't changed, that's why I'm antisocial—adults are people who can do what they like and no one reprimands them. I was very sensitive to the amorous intrigues of those around me, to the couples, to the adultery, so that when I read *Madame Bovary*, I identified with her completely, because she had money problems and so did I, and she secretly met her lover while I secretly went to the movies. And that is what gave me the urge in my films to show people in terrible trouble, because I had both the inclination to put myself in impossible situations and the capacity to suffer horribly in those situations, and that's basically why I like Hitchcock, because suspense is a horrible illness.

"Then, surprised that I had made a French film, although I had always admired American films, I make *Shoot the Piano Player* to pay my debt to American movies. But I realized I did not enjoy filming gangsters or violence. I found them boring. I didn't want to make heroes out of them or *Lavender Hill Mob* kind of inoffensive and funny gangsters, so I made my gangsters fantastic and promised myself—no more gangster movies.

"After that I made *Jules and Jim*. I had always loved the novel, written by a man 75 years old [Henri-Pierre Roché], about two friends in love with the same woman, and for me it was a morality tale, not something scabrous, and I made it that way, without any physical love scenes. I also liked the idea of making a movie as though I were an old man, because the author was telling a real story that had happened to him when he was 20, and now he was writing about it 50 years later, which gave him a marvelous detachment and serenity, and I wanted to make a movie in the past tense, as if it had all happened a long time ago.

"Then I went back to an original screenplay with *The Soft Skin* [the story of a middle-aged married man who is drawn into an affair with an air hostess and is killed by his wife]. It was a very clinical study of adultery, and it was considered disappointing. And it was, because the principal character was not as attractive as an adolescent. No one wanted to forgive him anything. The malaise of a man caught in a complicated situation was so strongly expressed that it embarrassed the spectator.

"Then someone told me the story of Ray Bradbury's novel, *Fahrenheit 451*, because I was saying science fiction is uninteresting and arbitrary. But when I was told, 'This is about a society where books are banned, and where the firemen, instead of putting out fires, burn the books that they find,' I wanted to make the movie, because I wanted to show books in difficulty, almost as if they were people in difficulty. It took me years to raise the money, and finally I had to make the picture in England, which was a serious handicap, but I kept the same idea. There were four or five book-burnings. In the first one you could see the books in piles of 10 and 20, while in the last one you could read the type as it was consumed by the flames, you could see the pages curling, and I wanted the audience to suffer as if it were seeing animals or people burning.

"After that, I wanted to make another movie with Jeanne Moreau, but I didn't want a love story, so I thought of a book I had read when I was 14, called *The Bride Wore Black*, about a woman who kills the five men responsible for the accidental shooting of her husband on their wedding day, and I wanted to film it like a fairy tale. It was a story about fatality, about men who had done something in their youth, and this bride had the mission of vengeance to carry out. I told Jeanne Moreau not to be tragic, to play it like a skilled worker with a job to do, conscientious and obstinate.

"Then I made *Stolen Kisses* because over the years I had neglected Jean-Pierre Léaud, and I wanted to take up the character he played in *The 400 Blows*. It was a film that made itself. We started without a plot, we had fun, we didn't expect anything. When I think of a movie it's always in very simple terms, but when I'm finished, I'm surprised to find it's different from what I expected. I think of all the things that could only be understood by a few friends, not necessarily jokes, but a lot of allusions that help me solve problems of direction. Take the scene where the old detective dies while he's on the telephone. That really happened to a famous Russian director; he collapsed and his secretary picked up the phone and said, 'Hang up, please, your party is dead.'

"Sometimes it's things I see around me. In the last scene of *Stolen Kisses*, a man comes up to Antoine and his girl and proposes her a definitive love. Some people interpreted that character as death, but it's just an idea I got in a restaurant, when I saw a man looking insistently at a woman who was with a date, and I told myself, 'It would be wonderful if he got up and declared himself.' I remembered that when I was looking for an ending. I didn't want a happy ending; I had to show that their happiness was threatened, and I immediately found the phrases the movie should end on; she said, 'But that man is mad,' and Antoine replied, 'Yes, yes,' but you sensed that he did not think so, that he was upset, because the whole film turns on what escapes you, what can't last.

"And I also liked the idea of a character for whom love is definitive, because there are a great many couples, one of whom considers that love is temporary while the other that it is definitive, and that is what creates the crisis of separation. There are many women who feel that the choice of a man is definitive.

"I work on location and never use a shooting script. We were going to shoot the last scene of *Jules and Jim* in a cottage on the edge of a forest, but when we got there, there was such a heavy fog we shot it outdoors in the fog, and later we got a call from John Frankenheimer who was making *The Train*; he wanted to know how we'd obtained such fantastic fog.

"I like to shoot on location because it's real. Studio doors don't close properly; I'm very attached to the truth of a door, the truth of a window, the truth of curtains. And when you go to real places, you can't prepare your script because you don't know what you're going to find, so you have to improvise. I like to use the time when the cameramen and the technicians are working, when the actors are putting on their make-up, that time when the director, if he's prepared everything, is twiddling his thumbs, to write my scenes. Everything works together: once I've seen the position of the chairs and the windows I see how the scene should unfold. I work better if I can write each scene at the last moment.

"I don't like the actors to arrive on the set knowing their dialogue by heart. I want them to learn it in the heat of the moment. I think when you're feverish, in the medical sense of the word, you're much sharper, and I want my films to give the impression they were made with a fever of 104. Some actors have trouble adjusting. In *Mississippi Mermaid*, a great friend of mine and a great actor, Michael Bouquet, who is so wonderful in Anouilh plays, arrived on location at Aix-en-Provence on a Monday, the only day he's not on stage, and I gave him his lines when he got off the plane, which gave him time to learn them between the airport and the set, and he came to me in a panic and said, 'François, I would do anything for you, I have the utmost confidence in you, but please, please, don't ask me to do this.' So I told him to come back the following Monday.

"Also, because of this, my dialogues are seldom more than a page or a page and a half, the scenes rarely last more than two minutes. In any case, that is not a real problem. What matters is that the failure of an interesting director is far more worthwhile than the success of a hack. Also, I've come around to an idea that I rejected when I was a critic, and that is to consider a film like a mayonnaise. All the ingredients might be good but it doesn't take, or a film can be totally different from what you intended because of an actor. But finally, what Giraudoux said is true, there are no good and bad plays, only good and bad play-wrights.

"Take Godard, for example, he makes two or three movies a year, because he works like a painter. For him, what counts is not a single movie, but the work he has done during a certain artistic period. What I admire most in his films (although he can, if he wants to, show that he is visually one of the world's best directors) is the beauty of his dia-logues. He started making movies at the time when we all discovered Bergman, who liberated dialogue, that is, he showed us that the charac-ters need only express what the director wants them to. There is no need to concern oneself with their psychology, or their social situation, or the plot.

"And Godard has secrets, you know, he never has a character go out a door and into the street. His characters go out a door, turn to the left, retrace their steps, and then go into the street. They put a cigarette into their mouth, take it out, put it back in, light it, and when it's lit, throw it away. He is the only one who is able to express the instability of life. And he has also done away with the notion of characters who are lik-able or not likable, because in his films there are no feelings.

"Godard is certainly the most imitated director in the world, and people say, 'He opened the doors,' but I don't think so. I think he opened the doors for him, just as it's very dangerous to imitate Orson Welles by placing the camera on the ground. That's O.K. for him but not for the rest of us.

"Antonioni is the only important director that I have nothing good to say about. He bores me; he's so solemn and humorless. And I don't like the way he deals with women, because instead of talking about them as a man would, he talks about them as thought he had been told their secrets, like General de Gaulle telling the Algerians, 'I have understood you.' He flatters women, but it doesn't seem authentic to me. I don't see the merit of so much gravity. In *Blow-Up* he was telling us, 'This is England today.' Well, that is a topic for journalists; I don't think it's very interesting for an artist to turn himself into a sociologist.

"The New Wave? Well, in the same three-month period in 1959 there came out Alain Resnais's *Hiroshima Mon Amour*, Chabrol's *The Cousins*, Marcel Camus's *Orfeo Negro*, and *The 400 Blows*. It was an event. In 30 years it will be impossible to write a history of the movies without mentioning the New Wave. I see it as a return to the origins of movies which in 1895 was a young art. You know when Méliès went to Louis Lumiere to buy the patent, Lumiere told him, 'I would be doing you a disservice, this thing has no future.' But Méliès believed in it, and after him there were a lot of young directors, until sound made movies too expensive to entrust to young people. The New Wave was a group of young people who had decided in their teens that they would make movies, whereas in the early days people got into movies by chance, because a neighbor was in it, or like Renoir, because he didn't want to be a painter like his father.

"That was our main link, that we got into movies by vocation and not by chance, that we started young, that we all learned the same lessons of simplicity and coherence from Renoir, Rossellini and Hitchcock, and that we wanted to assume entire responsibility for our films. And also, we were very conscious of the need for good acting. More than the others, I am concerned with the characters; I'm closer to the nineteenth century. There is not that much difference between a film I make and a novel that could have been published a hundred years ago.

"My characters are on the edge of society. I want them to testify to human fragility, because I don't like toughness. I don't like very strong people or people whose weaknesses don't show, and that rules out a number of actors with whom I can't work. I have allergies; I could never have made a movie with Clark Gable or John Wayne or an American-style hero. Jean-Paul Belmondo is my type of actor. He can say sad things magnificently; his voice in *Mississippi Mermaid* enchants me, and physically he is very special. He can play a handsome character or an ugly character; he is like a bottle which you can fill with whatever you want. It's stupefying, he has the widest range of any actor today; he can play Jean Gabin parts and Gerard Philipe parts; in fact, it's too bad they don't have anyone like him in the States. Steve McQueen is inter-esting because he's sensitive, he has blue eyes, he has a Gary Cooper side, but still his face is too brutal, and the motorcyclist in him bothers me. The trouble in the States is that so many actors today come from television where they've been hired to play G-men and spies. No one has replaced Jimmy Stewart or Spencer Tracy or Cary Grant, those gentle, clear-eyed actors.

"I don't like the term director; I don't direct actors, I shunt them. At first I let them do what they want, and I might leave it that way, or I'll say, 'Make it sadder.' With Belmondo it's hallucinating, you don't even have to interrupt the scene. He starts out in a comic vein and the dis-parity with what I want is so great that I tell myself, 'I'm going to have to explain this, it's going to be difficult, it's going to take a long time,' and not at all, he says, 'Oh, you want it sadder,' and within seconds he changes it completely. That's because he has the dual theater-movie training. He knows how to emphasize a line and how to throw a line away, whereas Catherine Deneuve is exclusively cinematic, completely untheatrical, every intonation is even. So sometimes you have to say, 'This sentence is important'; you have to bring her out.

"I think they go well together; they're good to look at. I made *Mississippi Mermaid* in Cinemascope, so I could have them both on the screen most of the time. In a lot of American movies with two big stars you have a problem of vanity; each star is filmed separately so you can put little lights in their eyes, and you get the impression they didn't act together. But I didn't want one to be more important than the other so I kept them together.

"I always take an actor aside so the rest of the crew can't hear what I'm saying. I believe in a muted, discreet method. I want the actors to forget there are a lot of people around; that's why I never allow any vis-itors or journalists on the set. In love scenes I ask the perchman to take his perch away and shoot it with a hidden microphone. All my inti-mate scenes are done with only four or five people around, with hardly any lighting. I almost never show lovemaking or kissing; either the kisses are interrupted, or you can't see the faces.

"I don't like kisses on the mouth, they distract me. I have the impres-sion when the scene is too physical that it's slowing down the movie. The physical side of love stories bothers me. In *Stolen Kisses* I showed a husband with a detective breaking in on his wife naked in bed with another man, but I tried to save the scene by having the detective hand the husband a vase of flowers to throw at them. But instead of throwing the vase he throws the flowers.

"I've only had real trouble with an actor once, and that was with Oskar Werner in *Fahrenheit*. I had never had a hero in a movie. I had always had characters whom I had to convince the public to like, even though they were in the wrong, like Jeanne Moreau who loves two men at the same time, or like the selfish and unconcerned piano player. With *Fahrenheit*, for the first time, I had a character who was in the right, because he came to the defense of books, so it bothered me, it was as if I was making a movie with Kirk Douglas. I felt uncomfortable with a positive character.

"I asked Oskar to forget the heroics and to play the part with a great deal of modesty. But he wanted to play it with arrogance, like someone who is right against everyone else. It was a misunderstanding from morning to night. We argued all the time, and he would arrive on the set in a bad mood, and I would say, 'Oskar, in that scene you look like you're sulking,' and he said, 'Not at all, it's a science-fiction film and I'm playing it like a robot, I have annihilated thought.' and I said, 'That's all well and good, but you'd be better off playing it like a monkey'—that is, I wanted him to discover books like an animal, for the first time, sniffing at them, wondering what they were.

"On top of that, he is strongly misogynist, and he was playing opposite Julie Christie in both parts of the wife and the young girl. I wanted him to be nice to his wife, to treat her as if she were ill, because she was against books. She thought they were dangerous as dynamite, but he said, 'No, she's a Nazi, I've got to insult her.' So I had to change a lot of scenes. I ended each scene with a close-up of Julie Christie and I told her, 'Look at him as though you are normal and he is very, very sick.'

"Then we came to the scenes with the poetic young girl, and he wanted to play the seducer. He touched her arms and her shoulders, because, he said, 'I'm not happy at home with my wife, so I want romance with this young girl.' I told him, 'That will be most unpleasant. This is not a movie about adultery, this is science fiction. Touching her is out of the question; it will be disgusting to see you being a brute at home with your wife and a Romeo away from home with this young girl.' But he did it his way; he constantly disobeyed, so I would get angry and say, 'I forbid you to touch her,' which made him furious, and we reached a point where we weren't even speaking to each other, and I would go through the scene with his stand-in, who told him what to do when he arrived. For the last three weeks of shooting we didn't say a word to each other.

"Well, those things happen. What shocks me is when I see a director, who has really suffered with an actor, make another movie with him—that's real servility. With *Fahrenheit*, if I hadn't waited six years to make it, I would have left like a shot.

"Often I write with a particular actor in mind. When I write for Jeanne Moreau I can hear her voice. We've been friends for 10 years. She has a kind of moral authority; even in a disgusting movie like *Great Catherine* it shines through. She is very physical, very carnal, but she prevents anything dirty from coming out over on the screen. She is like love; she is not like lechery, and she must feel that way herself because she is very firm about refusing to act in movies about adultery. She would never have played a part like Anne Bancroft in *The Graduate*. In *Jules and Jim* she rejects conventional morality, but invents her own, and it leads her to suicide. When you know her, you find that she has the qualities of both a man and a woman, without the laborious reasoning side of men and without the coquettishness of women.

"Some actors are able to change my conception of the characters I want them to play, like Jean-Pierre Léaud in *The 400 Blows*. I picked him from 60 children I interviewed. He wanted the part so badly; he had such vitality. I was thinking of a more introverted child, and I kept adapting the screenplay to suit him. In one scene, where the psychologist questions Antoine, I told him to answer what he wanted; it was improvised, and he even brought in a grandmother who was not in the rest of the film. People said we looked alike, and it may be true. And then, because we saw so much of each other, there was a mimetic thing.

"Also, his life was a little like my own, he had an unstable childhood. When we were shooting *The 400 Blows*, he was living with his parents, and his mother came to see me, weeping, and said, 'It's not possible, he wants to fight his father,' and then he would show up on the set with his face bruised. When you're making a picture you're very selfish, and

I said, 'This can't go on.' So I took him in. At that point, I toughened the movie; I decided it shouldn't be a comedy.

"The script-girl told me, 'You know, the public will never accept this move because you are showing them a little loafer who steals money and hides it in the chimney.' But when the movie came out, I had the opposite impression; I felt the public was too severe with the parents and too indulgent with Antoine. Because I had wanted to show that the parents were totally at a loss with this unpredictable kid, who does everything in hiding. But the way it came out, the child was adorable.

"The lack of success of *The Soft Skin* can be explained because the principal character is a kind of Monsieur Bovary. He lies to his wife; he takes his mistress with him on a lecture tour in the provinces, but he says, 'I can't show up in front of everyone with this girl,' and he hides her in a small hotel, whereas he has a room reserved in the biggest hotel. He only does monstrous, hypocritical things. It shocked a lot of people. But for me *The Soft Skin* is about the same thing as *The 400 Blows*. It shows a character caught in an ever-tightening web of circumstance. The audience could accept that kind of behavior from a child but not from a well-dressed, middle-aged man, responsible for his actions.

"In *Stolen Kisses* I was able to make the audience accept the fact that Antoine Doinel, now 20, could at the same time sleep with a girl his own age, with a married woman, and with whores. Even his worst misdeed is acceptable. When after the burial of the old detective he picks up a whore outside the cemetery, the audience accepts it because he's still an adolescent at heart and, of course, Léaud is like that as a person, full of goodwill and awkwardness, a combination of anguish and wholesomeness."

The Story of the Degradation of Love by Passion

YVONNE BABY / 1969

FT: I read the *Mississippi Mermaid* when I was adapting *The Bride Wore Black*. In that period, I read everything written by William Irish in order to be impregnated by his work and to be, in spite of the necessities of being cinematically unfaithful, to stay as close as possible to the novel. I very much like to know an author completely before I adapt his work to the screen. So when I am faced with an "Irish problem," I have the opportunity to find an "Irish solution." I proceeded in this manner with David Goodis for *Shoot the Piano Player* and with Ray Bradbury for *Fahrenheit 451*.

In *The Mermaid*, I admired, above all, the distribution of the events, the appearances, disappearances, and reappearances of the two principal characters. I therefore respected this construction for the film. I sought to conserve all the proportions.

Irish is part of those American authors who were influenced by the cinema. I became more conscious of this influence when I was adapting *The Mermaid*, and I worked on the book as if it were already a scenario. In the novel, Irish says of the detective, "He had the most direct look that one could ever encounter." This sole indication I gave to Michel Bouquet and that was enough for him to create the role.

My definitive screenplay was less of an adaptation in the traditional sense where one chooses the scenes. After all, I could realize the dream of all directors, to shoot in chronological order, a chronological story that represents an itinerary.

From *Le Monde*, 21 June 1969. Reprinted by permission of Yvonne Baby.

YB: *And what is this itinerary?*

FT: The same as the story. The shoot began on the island of Réunion, it continued to Nice, Antibes, Aix-en-Provence, Lyons, to finish in the snow near Grenoble.

The fact of respecting the chronology allowed me to "construct" the couple with precision. The plot is full of the romance of the previous century. I thought that it was necessary to parallel the emotional course of the novel (which we followed) with a physical course. That means that at each stage the spectator knows exactly where the characters are in their physical rapport as in their emotional rapport. It is perhaps by this that the film could appear in the category of a "film of love and adventure." Which describes a couple of today. The situation is exceptional but the characters are close to us.

YB: *Why did you choose Catherine Deneuve and Jean-Paul Belmondo?*

FT: Jean-Paul Belmondo, with Jean-Pierre Léaud, is my favorite actor. As for Catherine Deneuve, it was impossible for me not to think of her. In fact, her role in *The Mermaid* is an accumulation of various aspects of her which we have seen recently. For example her romantic side in *Benjamin*, and her "secret life" aspect in *Belle De Jour*. Besides, it is good to have in a film that is linked to a certain tradition of American cinema to have two stars of equal celebrity. But even though the Deneuve-Belmondo couple is superb there exists in Paris a certain prejudice regarding stars and that is an even stronger reason that they go in pairs. In New York, the view is different. I was there last year and when I spoke of *The Mermaid* to American journalists, they said to me, "Catherine Deneuve and Jean-Paul Belmondo are charming. They'll make a lovely couple."

And because Belmondo is the most complete European actor who alternates three characters in his career: that which originates from Sganarelle, that which is inspired by American gangster movies and that which could be the son of Jean Gabin in *La Bête Humaine* (*The Human Beast*). It is this third possibility that I asked of him, to explore and use his gravity, which allows him to say words of love.

YB: *So you've made another film about love?*

FT: Yes, but even if I have the reputation for making many films about love, I felt very clearly that, for the first time, I was making a film about a couple. In *The Mermaid* there is no second man or second woman and I was able to concentrate entirely on the intimacy of the couple. The passage of *voussoiement* (as Gide calls it) to *tutoiement* with the return to *voussoiement*, the confidences, the long silences, and those thorough tests and deceptions that take two people to become indispensable one to the other.

In *The Bride Wore Black* there are five crimes and here only one. *The Mermaid* is, above all, a story of the degradation of love by passion. I believe that the majority of my films are constructed on the principle of people being caught in a machine in which we find the protagonist always weaker than the partner. As usual, it's the heroine who takes the initiative. And equally, as usual, the story is recounted less visibly by the hero.

YB: *Why do you refer to* Johnny Guitar *in your film?*
FT: Because *Johnny Guitar* is a false Western just as *The Mississippi Mermaid* is a false adventure. My taste leads me to pretend to be submitting to Hollywood genres (melodramas, thrillers, comedies, etc.). In the interior of the constraints of these genres, I express a great freedom of action all along my work. For example, during the making of this film, which was almost that of a super-production, I permitted myself to write the dialogue of the next day each evening to profit even more from the psychological advantages that was offered me by shooting the film chronologically. The actors had just enough time to learn the text which I gave them at the last moment. Their surprise passing immediately into the scene was increased in intensity on seeing the reactions of the technical crew who discovered the sudden changes with them.

In this job, it is necessary to make progress and looking back on my more recent films, I have the impression that I have slightly neglected the visual aspect and which is even more serious, is that color is now become almost obligatory. I am therefore forced to pay greater attention to the photography, helped here by the extraordinary photogenic sky of Réunion and by the sensibility of my operator Denys Clerval. Yet, since *Jules and Jim,* I've never had such good conditions for shooting, and it seems to me that for *The Mermaid*, the talents are particularly well mixed, notably Antoine Duhamel, responsible for the music; or Yves Saint Laurent, to my knowledge the most cinephilic of all couturiers. Yves Saint Laurent really understood what is necessary for cinema costumes, taking into account both movement and style.

YB: *You dedicated* The Mississippi Mermaid *to Jean Renoir . . .*
FT: *Stolen Kisses* was dedicated to Henri Langlois because I made it at the time of the Cinémathèque affair. This one to Renoir because in my improvisational work, it was of him, as always, I thought. Faced with every difficulty, I asked myself "How would Renoir get out of it? For, I believe that a filmmaker can never feel alone, if he knows well the 36 films of the director of *The Rules of the Game* and *La Grande Illusion.*

Truffaut's Tenderness Tames His Wolf Boy

CLAUDE VEILLOT/1969

IN A GRASS-COVERED BACK courtyard of a small country manor in Limagne in the Auvergne, a man in shirtsleeves, seated on a straw chair, is playing the drums. Next to him a blind-folded boy. When the child identifies the sound of the drum and correctly imitates it, the man's lips open in a wide smile.

The man at the drums is François Truffaut. The child is Jean-Pierre Cargol, nephew of the illustrious guitarist Manitas de Plata: the small gypsy boy whom the director of *Stolen Kisses* chose among 250 others to play *The Wild Child*, the wolf-boy discovered in the Rouergue at the end of the eighteenth century and whose re-education the film evokes.

It is six years exactly since *The 400 Blows*, and *The Wild Child* marks a return to source. It will be a "true" Truffaut to make one forget the semi-failure of his American adaptations such as *The Bride Wore Black* and *The Mississippi Mermaid*.

The role of Victor, the wild child, is one of the most difficult ever for a 12-year-old boy. That's why François Truffaut decided to take the role of Dr. Jean Itard himself, the educator of Victor, the wolf-boy of the Aveyron.

"The essential part of the film is how the man shows the little savage how to climb stairs, open a door, put on shoes, hold a spoon . . . It is a constant manipulation of the child. During the different attempts with the actors, but also non-professionals, I felt it was never going to be easy. I felt frustrated. It was better that I played the role myself."

From *L'Express*, 18 August 1969. Reprinted by permission of *L'Express*.

It was the same intuition that pushed him in *The 400 Blows* to interrogate Jean-Pierre Léaud for the celebrated scene with the psychologist, which he dubbed later with a woman's voice. Once we have seen Truffaut training the small Victor with an attentive authority, inventing for him the pathetic educative games, attempting to get him to pronounce certain sounds, one can picture the serious benevolence of Jean Itard. Certain ideas, disconcerting at first, become evident. Without doubt, because *The Wild Child* will respond to the profound preoccupations of its director, who is putting so much of himself into it. "I've been thinking of this film for five years," he says. "Ever since I read *Memoir of the rapport of Victor de l'Aveyron*, published in 1806, and republished in the book by Lucien Malson, *The Wild Children, myth and reality*. The legend of Romulus and Remus, that of Mowgli, that of Tarzan are there to remind us how alive is the myth of a child abandoned in nature and trying to survive. The story of Victor de Aveyron is even more fascinating, because it's absolutely authentic."

It was in 1797 that the wild child was seen for the first time wandering nude in the woods, fleeing humans, climbing trees, and walking on all fours. One didn't know how a child could have survived in a forest for eight years. Captured in 1798, brought to Paris, he excited public curiosity for a time; however, they were soon disappointed by this small dejected creature, incapable of speech, and in his look which, as Itard wrote, "seemed to slide over objects never fixing on them."

For Phillipe Pinel, the most famous journalist of the time, the child was just a classic idiot, identical to those kept in Bicêtre Hospital. His young colleague Itard, doctor-in-chief at the Institution for the deaf and mute, felt that the exterior signs of idiocy came not from a logical deficiency but from a natural insufficiency. The child was entrusted to Itard, who took him into his home, gave him the name of Victor, and with the help of a governess, attempted his education.

Truffaut and his co-scenarist Jean Gruault wrote *The Wild Child* to approach the theme of communication. Specialists admit today that Jean Itard "described and treated a psychotic child a century and a half before psychiatrists defined the state of mind," and we should consider him equally as a pioneer of the education of social inadequates.

"Basically," pondered Truffaut, "I always relate stories of a lack, a frustration. *The 400 Blows* was the lack of tenderness. *Fahrenheit 451*, the lack of culture. *The Wild Child* is the frustration of knowledge, with Itard's obstinately attempting to eliminate the lack. He wrote in his memoir, 'Without civilization, man would be the weakest and least intelligent of animals.' It's a film on communication, exchange, language, and culture."

The film, for which Artistes Associés have been prepared to supply most of the means, is being shot far from Paris, in black and white, at Truffaut's insistence, with only three principal characters and a reduced crew.

While the director lunches on a peach, in the shade of the camera, two of his favorite scenarists, Claude de Givray and Bernard Revon, are trying out the food in a neighboring inn, preparing *Bed and Board*, more of the imaginary biography of Antoine Doinel, the hero of *The 400 Blows* and *Stolen Kisses*.

"I like very much to make a film and discuss the next one at the same time. Givray, Revon, and I exchange ideas, I take notes . . . It helps me to relax before going to sleep." While Truffaut is talking, the small Jean-Pierre Cargol comes up to him and hugs him. Truffaut twists the boy's ear and pulls affectionately at his hair, calling him "my flea." And if the director moves away for a moment from the place of filming, it's not rare to hear the voice of the little actor shouting, "Where are you, my Truffaut?"

It is like a prolongation of the story of *The Wild Child*. The almost fanatical love that the small interpreter has for Truffaut, is the ultimate and just recompense for Truffaut's tenderness.

François Truffaut

CHARLES THOMAS SAMUELS/1970

THE IMAGE PRESENTED when François Truffaut played the
principle role in *The Wild Child*—that of a short, compactly built, but
expressionless and ordinary-looking young man in his late thirties—
leaves out his most striking features: a smile no less charming than his
most charming films and the continuous glint of risible interest in his
eyes. Truffaut's quick lucidity made him the ideal interview subject.
Even when he had to interrupt an answer to await translation (he
speaks no English), he never lost the thread. Nor did he ever hesitate or
appear to find any question unexpected.

The interview took place in two sessions at Les Films du Carrosse, the
production company he founded and runs. In his private office and
throughout a small suite in the same building where *Bed and Board* was
filmed, the atmosphere is literally one of "quiet elegance." The firm is
clearly busy, but the employees seem to be running a doctors' consor-
tium rather than a movie company.

During the period when I met Truffaut, he was attending to every
detail of the press premiere of *Bed and Board*, prior to attending the
Lincoln Center opening of *The Wild Child*. He invited me to the screen-
ing, where he greeted each guest personally. When, on the next day,
I arrived for the interview, Truffaut was equally hospitable to me and
particularly to my friend, Mme. Françoise Longhurst, who acted as
translator. During the conversation, growing rapport made translation

---

progressively dispensable. Eventually, we began to respond to each other directly, joking away an occasional contretemps in our mutual involvement in the give-and-take.

SAMUELS: *You began your career as a critic. What effect has this had on you as a director?*
TRUFFAUT: It is difficult to say, because one looks at films differently when one is a director or a critic. For example, though I have always loved *Citizen Kane*, I loved it in different ways at different stages of my career. When I saw it as a critic, I particularly admired the way the story is told: the fact that one is rarely permitted to see the person who interviews all the characters, the fact that chronology is not respected, things like that. As a director I cared more about technique: All the scenes are shot in a single take and do not use reverse cutting; in most scenes you hear the soundtrack before you see the corresponding image—that reflects Orson Welles's radio training—etc. Behaving like the ordinary spectator, one uses a film as if it were a drug; he is dazed by the motion and doesn't try to analyze. A critic, on the other hand (particularly one who works for a weekly, as I did), is forced to write summaries of films in fifteen lines. That forces one to apprehend the structure of a film and to rationalize his liking for it.

S: *Are there any critics you particularly admire or, as a director, have found particularly useful?*
T: No filmmaker likes critics, no matter how nice they are to him. Always he feels that they didn't say enough about him, or that they didn't say nice things in an interesting way, or that they said too many of their nice things about other directors. Since I was a critic, I am perhaps less hostile to critics than other directors are. Nevertheless, I never consider the critic more than a single element in the reception of my films. The attitude of the public, publicity material, post-premiere ads: all these things are as important as critics.

S: *There are two traditions in film. One, ultimately derived from silent film, emphasizes editing and camera movement. The other—which Andre Bazin seems to have preferred (and which he exemplified with a film like William Wyler's* The Little Foxes*)—is more theatrical, depends on staging. Now your* *closeness to Bazin is well known. However, I think that you are not only less theatrical than the directors he professed to admire but that, indeed, your camera work and editing are more varied than that of any director of equal stature. If this is so, did Bazin have the influence on you which he is widely assumed to have had?*

T: I don't agree with the distinction you've made. Furthermore, Bazin overestimated *The Little Foxes*, which was just photographed theater—though it gave him a pretext for some interesting observations on the cinema. I would rather see a distinction made between filmmakers who attempt to keep the camera invisible—as John Ford did—and those who make it evident to the spectator.

S: *All right. But your camera was once extremely visible and now is becoming less so. Why?*

T: Because it became more visible in everyone else. No, I have a better reason: I have become more interested in my characters, in their situations, and in what they say.

S: *As a critic, you attacked vigorously the films made by French directors during the period before the so-called New Wave. What made them so hateful to you?*

T: I attacked them because they didn't have either a personal vision of life or of cinema.

S: *But some of them created great films. Isn't that admirable? Or do you deny the greatness of a film like Carné's* Children of Paradise *or Clement's* Forbidden Games?

T: I first became interested in films during the war, and therefore the first films I saw were native. I liked *Children of Paradise*, all the Carné-Prevert films—I even liked *The Night Visitors*, though I don't anymore. I liked the films of Becker, Clouzot's *The Raven*, and, of course, above all, the films of Renoir. Then there was the shock of the American films after the liberation. I saw them when I was thirteen or fourteen and in random order, without knowing which were made during and which after the war. I found them all richer than French films—except the best of ours, like *Children of Paradise* and the films of Renoir.

S: *I share your enthusiasm for six or seven Renoir films, but I've always been surprised at the extent of your admiration for him because though Renoir certainly made several first-rate films, it seems to me that some of his are even faultier than Carné's. They are even more theatrical—I think of a film like* Chotard and Company. *And then there is that awful sentimentality toward the French peasants, as in* Toni.

T: No, I adore *Toni*; it is a very important film for me.

S: *Why?*

T: Because a filmmaker always thinks that his films aren't close enough to real life, and *Toni* shows how to attain that closeness. It is like a news item; its atmosphere is so real; there is a sort of madness in its events that one does not find in a novel or short story but only in something from real life. Because, you know, even when you start with something from real life, it gets theatrical when translated into a scenario, and then the reality is gone.

S: *Precisely. Reality is what I find gone in* Toni. *Let me give you an example: In order to seduce Toni, the heroine pretends to have been bitten by a bee and asks him to suck the stinger out. Naturally, while doing so, his passion rises. That seems to me a theatrical cliché—perhaps not in all its details, but in its essentials.*

T: It is a cliché of love, not a cliché of drama. Perhaps you would find this banal if you merely read the script. But the way it's done, the way the actors play it, makes it real.

S: *You agree that the scene is banal in conception, but you think it's redeemed by the acting. That raises an interesting parallel to your own films. For example, in* Mississippi Mermaid, *when Deneuve and Belmondo leave a movie theater where they have just seen* Johnny Guitar, *they agree that the reality of the performances transformed that horse opera into a story of real people. Wasn't that your intention in* Mississippi Mermaid *and many other films: to take a banal idea and cause the actors to give it real life?*

T: Yes. Yes. Certainly.

S: *Do you think Deneuve and Belmondo did save the story?*

T: Yes. Whatever is wrong with that film is my fault and not the fault of my stars.

s: *Like many American critics, I'm surprised by your admiration for Howard Hawks and John Ford. Would you explain why you like them?*

t: Originally, I didn't like Ford—because of his material: for example, the comic secondary characters, the brutality, the male-female relationships typified by the man's slapping the woman on the backside. But eventually I came to understand that he had achieved an absolute uniformity of technical expertise. And his technique is the more admirable for being unobtrusive: His camera is invisible; his staging is perfect; he maintains a smoothness of surface in which no one scene is allowed to become more important than any other. Such mastery is possible only after one has made an enormous number of films. Questions of quality aside, John Ford is the Simenon of directors. Hawks, on the other hand, is the greatest cinematic intelligence among American directors. He isn't a cinema addict, nor is he anguished or obsessed. Rather, he loves life in all its manifestations, and because of this harmony with life in general, he was able to make the two or three greatest examples of every genre of film (except perhaps comedy, in which you have Lubitsch, etc.). To be specific: Hawks made the three best Westerns (*Red River*, *The Big Sky*, and *Rio Bravo*), the two best aviation films (*Only Angels Have Wings* and *Air Force*), and the three best thrillers (*The Big Sleep*, *To Have and Have Not*, and *Scarface*).

s: *M. Truffaut, Hawks's very versatility might be called an indication that he lacks a single vision of life or of cinema. Yet it is precisely that lack which you condemn in your French predecessors.*

t: But Hawks does have a vision of life and cinema! For example, he is the first American director to show women as equal to men (think of his handling of Lauren Bacall vis-à-vis Humphrey Bogart in *The Big Sleep*). He always knows what he is doing. When he decided to make *Scarface*, realizing the danger of a film about sordid mobsters, he instructed his scriptwriter, Ben Hecht, to join him in constantly thinking about the history of the Borgias so as to give the film some tragic stature. It is to this that we owe the nearly incestuous love between George Raft* and his sister in the film.

---

*Truffaut is mistaken. It is Paul Muni.

S: *With the exception of* Jules and Jim *you usually adapt trash novels to the screen. Why?*

T: I have often been asked to direct great novels, like Camus' *L'Etranger*, Fournier's *Le Grand Meaulnes*, Celine's *Voyage au bout de la nuit*, and *Du cote de chez Swann*. In each case my admiration for the book prevented me from making it into a film. *Jules and Jim* was an exception because it was so little known, and I wanted to increase its popularity by calling to it the attention of a large audience. However, despite what you say, I have never used a trash novel or a book I did not admire. Writers like David Goodis (author of *Down There*, the basis for *Shoot the Piano Player*) and William Irish (source for *The Bride Wore Black* and *Mississippi Mermaid*) have special value, and they have no counterparts in France. Here detective story writers are rotten, whereas in America writers as great as Hemingway work in that field. But because so many books appear each year in the States, these detective story writers are usually ignored. Ironically, this liberates them. Made humble by their neglect, they are free to experiment because they think no one is paying attention anyway. Not expecting to be analyzed, they put into their books anything they choose.

S: *I hadn't thought of that. Therefore, they reflect life as a muddle— incomprehensible variety. You see life that way, too, don't you?*

T: Yes. But let me tell you something. After seeing *Shoot the Piano Player* and liking it, Henry Miller was asked to write an introduction for a new edition of *Down There* and therefore had to read the book. He then phoned me to say that he suddenly realized that whereas my film was good, the book was even better. So you see, I don't film trash.

S: *In an interview you gave Louis Marcorelles, you said that people shouldn't distinguish art films from the more commercial product, that the only true distinction was between good films and bad. Is that a correct quotation?*

T: Yes.

S: *But don't some directors force one to make the distinction that you deplore? In France, one thinks of Bresson, who is a great artist but whose films fail at the box office.*

T: Commercial success is a result, never an intention. For example, Orson Welles never succeeded either, only one out of every two films Bunuel makes earns much money, etc.

S: *Well, then . . .*

T: Well, in America I still think that you simplify this issue. You say that Hollywood films are commercial and New York films are artistic. That is wrong.

S: *No doubt! There is a fascinating tension in your films. In most of them, the hero yearns for and searches after security while your technique keeps showing us that nothing in the world is safe or permanent. Am I right?*

T: Exactly. In fact, I said much the same thing in *Le Figaro* apropos my latest film, *Bed and Board.*

S: *Leave* Bed and Board *out of it for a moment. It also seems to me that your technique hasn't been so redolent of insecurity lately.*

T: Perhaps. But then for me life lately hasn't been so cruel!

S: *Another constant in your films has been the subject of love. I'm not asking you to be a philosopher, but are you aware of some settled notion about love that recurs in your thinking or feeling about it and that you reflect in your work?*

T: I have no ideas on this subject, only sensations, nothing more than I put in my films.

S: *Whenever you treat erotic passion, you keep it distant, never allowing us to see it closely. Why?*

T: I don't know.

S: *Music is terribly important in your films. How do you choose a composer? After you've chosen him, how much control do you exercise over his work?*

T: Actually, I am moving away from music in my films, like other directors (consider Bunuel and Bergman), who no longer use it at all. Still, it's not always possible to do without music completely, and I don't always like what I have. I like the music in *The 400 Blows* and *Shoot the Piano Player* but am not crazy about the music in *Jules and Jim.* The music in *The Soft Skin* and *Fahrenheit 451* is excellent, less so in *The Bride Wore Black. Stolen Kisses* has a wonderful score, as does *The Wild Child.* But the score of *Mississippi Mermaid* isn't very good, and that in *Bed and Board* is simply awful.

s: *Now that you have made this rundown, can you generalize about the qualities that appeal to you in movie music?*
T: It's very difficult to say. I like music to flow as uninterruptedly as the images. No, it's too difficult to express. Well, I suppose I can say that music shouldn't stop a film, which is what happens when the score is nonmelodic. For example, if you use jazz or pop music, the effect is anti-narrative.

s: *You've said that you never completely plan a film in advance and therefore improvise a good deal. What do you rely on to discipline your improvisations?*
T: The dialogue and the actors. I try to create units of emotion. That's why, for example, I filmed each scene of *Bed and Board* in a single take.

s: *Don't you also try to play each unit of emotion off against the next one?*
T: Exactly. Yes, that's absolutely true. For example, one of my favorite moments in *Bed and Board* is when Antoine enters the apartment after a visit to his Japanese girlfriend and the camera cuts from his astonished face to his wife, who is dressed and seated in traditional Japanese style. The audience laughs. But when the camera closes in on her face, we see her tears, and this shocks the spectator. It is precisely this kind of emotional contrast that I love.

s: *The acting in your films is usually extremely natural, but the situations in which the people find themselves are very formulaic. Is this a deliberate goal?*
T: Yes . . . how shall I answer this? One proceeds always by contrasts. If the situation is extraordinary, then one must force the actors to be naturalistic, and vice versa. But this is something one cannot reflect upon; it is completely instinctive.

s: The 400 Blows *is often compared to* Zero for Conduct. *Do you think this film or its director, Jean Vigo, influenced you?*
T: Jean Vigo went further than anyone—even than Renoir—in achieving real, crude, natural images. For that reason, we French directors speak of a secret that Vigo possessed and that we long to fathom. In my opinion, the one who has fathomed it most completely is Godard, and *Breathless* is the closest in spirit to Vigo of any recent French film. The

only reason Vigo was invoked so often apropos of *The 400 Blows* is that there are so few French films dealing with children that whenever one appears people are immediately reminded of *Zero for Conduct*. I was equally influenced, as a matter of fact, by the films of Rossellini and above all by *Germany: Year Zero*, which I greatly admire.

s: The 400 Blows *is very episodic. Were any of the episodes introduced during shooting?*
t: No. We followed the script without deviation.

s: *Why did you include in* The 400 Blows *that little "guest" scene between Jean-Claude Brialy and Jeanne Moreau?*
t: Brialy was a good friend of mine and offered to pass through the film, bringing Moreau with him. Since I knew and admired her work as a stage actress, I was very happy to agree.

s: *This sort of thing occurs very often in your films. For example, one of your colleagues from your film company appears both in* Mississippi Mermaid *(where he plays Belmondo's business partner) and in* Bed and Board. *In the latter film Helen Scott, who was your interpreter with Hitchcock, makes a brief appearance. And I could go on. Why do you do this?*
t: Why not?

s: *Very funny! How about giving me a more serious answer. You realize that you've been greatly criticized for this. Critics have said you're playing a childish game, rubbing the noses of your viewers in their ignorance of your life, private tastes, etc. Do you just say* merde *is this criticism, or do you have some defense of this practice?*
t: It's ridiculous to criticize this. The public isn't aware that I am putting my friends into my films. Only the few people who are aware question what I am doing. Moreover, I would never do it if I thought it might harm my story in any way. On the contrary, while writing I sometimes think, "This character is just like X. Why not have X play the role?"

s: *But it isn't only putting your friends into your films; it's all the references to other films—like having Belmondo in* Mississippi Mermaid *recuperate at a clinic named Heurtebise, which alludes to Cocteau's* Orpheus.

T: What difference does it make to the public if the clinic is called Heurtebise or Smee. It doesn't detract for anyone ignorant of the allusion, and it adds for someone who recognizes it. But those who know how I operate and perceive ten allusions in one of my films are so terrified that they've missed ten others that out of their own vanity they condemn this whole game—which, by the way, is not unique to me.

S: *In* The 400 Blows *how do you want us to react to the scene in which Antoine whirls in the centrifuge? That scene has inspired sharply contrasting interpretations.*
T: I didn't think of the reaction the public was going to have. I simply wanted to show a child in a situation that was new to him and because I wanted to avoid clichés—say, showing him on a roller coaster—I chose the centrifuge.

S: In The 400 Blows, *during that marvelous interview with Antoine and the psychologist, why don't you show the psychologist?*
T: The scene had to be improvised. I began by filming a 16 mm version in which I asked Léaud (who plays Antoine) questions, and he replied spontaneously. When we reached this scene in the actual shooting, I decided that what we were getting was inferior to my 16 mm trial, which had been so fresh. To regain that freshness, I adopted a peculiar method of working. I told everyone to leave the set except Leaud and the cameraman. Then I read out the scripted psychologist's questions, asking Léaud to answer on the spot with whatever came into his mind. During postsynchronization, I had my questions read over by the actress who played the psychologist. However, since I wanted a woman with a very soft voice, who by this time was very pregnant and therefore reluctant to be filmed, I had only her voice but not her person, so you hear and don't see her.

S: *Is this why the scene is full of interior dissolves?*
T: Exactly. Since when I originally filmed the scene, I had banished the script girl and clapper boy from the set, I had no one to mark the precise moments of cutting and thus had to use the relatively imprecise dissolve to mark all connections between the pieces of Léaud's response that I decided to retain.

S: The 400 Blows *ends with the famous freeze shot of Antoine, but that freeze is frequently anticipated in the film. For example, there are freezes of Antoine when the mother comes to school and learns that Antoine had said she was dead, when Antoine is being photographed by the police, when he is looking after his retreating friend in the reformatory sequence, etc. Was this motif intentional? If so, it indicates that, as it were, Antoine's end was fated.*

T: I had no such plan. Moreover, a freeze like the one at the police station is simply the result of showing a still photograph. And the final freeze was an accident. I told Leaud to look into the camera. He did, but quickly turned his eyes away. Since I wanted that brief look he gave me the moment before he turned, I had no choice but to hold on it: hence the freeze.

S: *The opening scene in* Shoot the Piano Player *tells us that the film will shift back and forth between lighter and darker emotions. Isn't it also an introduction to your theme?*

T: I don't know. No, it comes from Goodis. When I make a film by a writer, I like to read all his books. That scene you refer to occurs in another Goodis novel. I just thought it belonged there.

S: *Why?*

T: It's lifelike and striking. It establishes the film's tone.

S: *As I said. But in it the two characters discuss the definition of love, which points to your subject. Without that scene the audience could feel they were seeing a mere gangster story.*

T: I suppose so. You know when I film a gangster story, I feel safe: I know that the images will create the plot so that the dialogue can concentrate on love. On the other hand, when I take a story that is about love, I have to force it into a detective story mold. This is what I pushed to an extreme in *The Bride Wore Black*. We know that the heroine has to kill five men, so there is no plot suspense. Instead, I create suspense about character by not having the heroine ever discuss her motives. She goes to each place, says nothing, and the man courts her.

s: *I'm happy to hear you say that. I never thought this film was properly understood. I always thought it was about the meaning of love.*

T: It is a film that illustrates five different ways of comporting oneself with a woman.

s: *All of them bad, which is why she becomes a sort of avenging angel striking men down in behalf of her sex.*

T: Exactly.

s: *That is why each murder reflects the victim. For example, victim number one has no capacity for fidelity. On the day of his wedding, he is capable of being drawn to a balcony, where he has no business being, because he wants to flirt with Moreau, who is standing there. This allows her to push him off. The third victim, whose wife is away, wants to be closeted with her so they can make love, but he first has to get rid of his son. Therefore, she can persuade him to play hide-and-seek and, during the game, can wall him in a closet.*

T: Yes, but all those details are in the novel. Only the characterization originates with me.

s: *In that first murder, when we have a shot of her scarf floating down, did you mean thereby to block our disapproval of her, since the shot is so lyrical and makes the audience feel pleasant?*

T: No. It was completely accidental. I had thought the scarf would fall very quickly. By chance that day the air current caused it to fall very slowly and in gentle movements. I liked that, and so I followed it all the way to the ground.

s: *Did you mean the character played by Charles Denner to be a latent homosexual?*

T: I don't know.

s: *In* Shoot the Piano Player *when Charlie and Lena are walking together for the first time and he is trying to decide whether to make a pass, you have his conscience speak in a voice different from his own. Why?*

T: Because Charles Aznavour's voice is too authoritative to be appropriate at that moment.

S: *Another odd effect: When the owner of the bar informs on Charlie, you show him in three oval frames, panning across them. Why?*

T: I don't think that worked. Maybe it could have been taken out.

S: *I don't understand the editing in the love scene between Lena and Charlie. The pattern of cuts and dissolves is obscure.*

T: I wanted to give the impression of passing time and, again, because Aznavour's voice is too authoritative, I didn't want him to speak in the scene. So I took bits of Lena speaking and used the transitions you mentioned to unite them.

S: *Yes, but there are elisions in the time sequence, which is also, unless I'm mistaken, sometimes scrambled.*

T: Now I remember. I wanted to give the impression that they sleep, get up, talk, go back to sleep, get up, etc., etc. That's why it seems as you say.

S: *If you had to give an account of the meaning of this film, what would you say?*

T: I made *Shoot the Piano Player* completely without reflection. When people first saw it, they said, "Why did you make a film about such a disgusting lowlife?" but I never posed this question to myself. You see, I love *Down There* very much. I am always drawn by the fairy tale aura of the American detective novel—as I also was in *The Bride Wore Black*. Both films are like Cocteau films, mixing elements that are typically American and typically French and thus achieving an effect that is timeless, without country . . .

S: *Not of this world.*

T: Exactly. Well put. Not of this world. That's what I want. When Godard saw *Shoot the Piano Player*, he said this is the first film laid in a country of imagination. I don't think one should say at the beginning of a film, "This takes place in a purely imaginary world," because then the audience will certainly feel let down since they will expect too much. But the audience should be made to feel gradually, while watching the film, that they are in no certain place.

S: *In* Jules and Jim, *what do you think of Catherine?*
T: She is totally fabulous. If you met such a woman in real life, you would see in her only faults—which the film ignores.

S: *Not at all. In fact, many critics—at least in America—asserted that Catherine was a witch, a neurotic, a man-eater.*
T: You know what a French psychiatrist said: "*Jules and Jim* is about two children in love with their mother."

S: *As far as you're concerned, why does Catherine kill Jim?*
T: Because it happens in the last pages of the novel. Even the casket in the flames comes from the book. Everything I show is from the novel. I can't say why she killed him because the book doesn't say. It isn't a psychological novel. It is simply a love story that started and finished. If there is one difference between film and book, it is that the film is more puritanical. You see I was under thirty when I made it, whereas the novel's author was a man of seventy-three.

S: *Why did you put in the book-burning sequence?*
T: Because Jim is German, and that is the Reichstag fire. So far as I was concerned, that marks the end of an epoch—an epoch of artists and dilettantes. Moreover, it prepares us for the burning of Jim and Catherine which ends the film.

S: *Yes. This historical dimension is very important in the film. Isn't that why each successive scene includes a Picasso from a later period? Isn't that the way you mark time?*
T: Yes.

S: *This film is full of photographs, this story is full of stories. Why?*
T: *Jules and Jim* was an autobiographical novel, written fifty years after the events reported in it. What I admired about the book was not only the story, but the temporal distance, which I had somehow to render on film. Thus I rarely shot the characters in close-up, and when I did, I tried to give full-length views. I wanted the film to look like an album of old photographs.

S: *You so often answer my questions about your intentions by saying you do what you do to be faithful to the novel you are adapting. What about* Fahrenheit 451, *which is very untrue to the spirit of its source? Ray Bradbury's novel is an allegory about the McCarthy era, highly political in its theme. Were you aware of this? In any case, why doesn't the political dimension appear in your film?*

T: It is not the sort of thing that interests me. I usually make films from books I admire, as I've told you. *Fahrenheit 451* was different. One day I was having a conversation with a friend about science fiction, which I told him I didn't like because it is too far from reality, too arbitrary in its events, incapable of rousing any emotions in me. In rebuttal, my friend told me of the plot of Bradbury's book, describing a society in which books were forbidden, in which firemen did not put out fires but set them in order to burn books, in which men who wanted to read were forced to commit the text to memory. When I heard all this, I instantly decided to make the film, but I had not actually read the novel.

S: *Do you have a special feeling for books?*

T: No. I love them and films equally, but how I love them! When I first saw *Citizen Kane*, I was certain that never in my life had I loved a person the way I loved that film. My feeling is expressed in that scene in *The 400 Blows* where Antoine lights a candle before the picture of Balzac.

S: *You say that politics didn't interest you as a theme for* Fahrenheit 451. *But though the reference is different from Bradbury's, your film does have a slight suggestion of political allegory. The firemen wear quasi-Nazi uniforms, Oskar Werner has a thick German accent, and anyone who comes to the film after seeing* Jules and Jim *sees in the earlier film's newsreel sequence about the Reichstag fire a sort of model for* Fahrenheit 451.

T: Originally, *Fahrenheit 451* was to have been made in France with Jean-Paul Belmondo. I couldn't find financing here and so had to shoot the film in England with Oskar Werner, who had not been my first choice for the starring role. I did want an actor of his type—one more poetic than psychological—but I did not want an actor with a German accent. During the shooting I kept telling him to play Montag gently; he decided to play the man as a Nazi.

S: *Beginning with* Fahrenheit, *the influence of Hitchcock seems to make itself felt. Is that why you made a studio film and used back projection in the Hitchcock manner?*

T: That has nothing to do with Hitchcock. We were in England, yet I wanted to show the French countryside. Consequently, I had to shoot in a studio and project the French countryside on a screen behind the action.

S: *I have the impression that this film began to bore you while you were making it. The first fifteen minutes are utterly successful: tense and moving. Later you dissipate the tension by little jokes that seem to subvert the film's seriousness. For example, when Cyril Cusack (the chief) leads the firemen in a book search in a park, he finds a minuscule book in a baby's pram and wags a finger at the child. Later, when Montag has begun to read and is rejected by the firepole (which men go up rather than down), Cusack turns to him and says, "What's this, Montag, something wrong between you and the pole?" At the end of the film, when we meet the book people who have "become" books, a set of twins appears, one named Pride, the other Prejudice. And so on.*

T: Ha-ha. You know it is oppressive for me to make a film on a "big subject." I found this film lacking in humor and so put in those jokes you mention. But perhaps some of them are wrong. You see, if I had done the film in French, I would have had complete control of the language; in English, I never quite knew if a line was right. Making *Fahrenheit* is what taught me that dialogue was more important in a film than I had realized. It is, in fact, the most important thing. With images, if they are good, one attains seventy percent of possible satisfaction; with good dialogue, one attains perhaps ninety percent. The most personal of attributes is one's fingerprint; dialogue is the fingerprint of a film. In *Fahrenheit 451* I was blocked by my imperfect control over the dialogue, and therefore, I was frustrated. Since then, you will note, all my films have a lot of dialogue in them.

S: *Since you like dialogue so much, why don't you write plays?*

T: I am bothered by the theater. The performance is not the same every night. Besides, I hate to talk to several people at once.

S: *I can't find any significance in* The Soft Skin. *It seems almost a documentary.*

T: But a documentary powerfully dramatized!

S: *I wonder about that and about numerous implausibilities. Why should so lovely a girl be attracted by the middle-aged hero, Lachenay?*

T: But that is very normal. In life one never stops wondering what someone sees in someone else.

S: *All right. I accept the fact that she falls in love with him, but can I believe that she spends all those hours sitting in a restaurant listening to him lecture about Balzac?*

T: Even an unappealing man becomes appealing when he discusses his work. That's why I made him discuss Balzac not in a scholarly way but as if he were describing a football match. His profound involvement in his subject moves her.

S: *Do you think Françoise Dorléac listens in that way?*

T: She needn't show her interest. She is a girl of the twentieth century impressed by a man of the nineteenth.

S: *The film is full of uneventful shots of objects. Were you trying to establish a certain style with this mute realism?*

T: That didn't give a style to the film; it is its style.

S: Stolen Kisses *seems more improvisational than your other films.*

T: It was.

S: *How did the improvisations take place? Were you or Léaud their guiding spirit?*

T: The improvisations were forced on both of us because of the desperate state I was in when the film was made. Nothing worked. I had already written *The Wild Child* and *Mississippi Mermaid*, yet I was shackled to a rotten project. I got into it because I had wanted to make another film with Léaud but couldn't find any material. We began with a vacuum that had to be filled. We said, "Let him have a sweetheart, let him have an affair with a married woman, let him work for a detective agency, etc."

S: *What did you rely on to hold it all together?*

T: Léaud. There are actors who are interesting even if they merely stand in front of a door; Léaud is one of them.

S: *One of the best scenes in* Stolen Kisses *occurs when the homosexual comes to the detective in search of his missing boyfriend. One hand, which is gloved, caresses the other, suggesting subtly but brilliantly the nature of the man.*

T: The gesture was improvised. We hit on it naturally because everything about that character needed to be bizarre.

S: *It's particularly interesting because the homosexual's love is both more powerful and more moving than the normal affairs of Antoine.*

T: But this is a true story which a friend learned while interviewing a detective. The dentist in the film is also taken from real life. Everything in that film is true.

S: *One of the film's most striking scenes shows Antoine looking into the mirror and chanting the names of the two women in his life. How did you hit on this idea?*

T: I needed to show that Antoine was torn between them, but there was no other character in the film whom he could talk to. Therefore, I had him talk to himself.

S: *It is very charming. But, you know, many people hold that sort of charm against you. They say you calculate such effects simply to please, with one eye cocked at the audience.*

T: But the scene isn't charming. It is long and makes people uneasy. In Germany, they cut it.

S: *But what about the general point?*

T: The role of Antoine is so close both to me and to Jean-Pierre Léaud that we never think of other people. For example, Antoine never quarrels with anyone in the films because I am the same way. If a quarrel begins, I simply leave.

S: *Is that why you don't correct misinterpretations of your work?*

T: In *The 400 Blows* I thought I had presented the parents and Antoine very naturally. The parents were guilty of showing so little

love, but, after all, Antoine was very difficult. Then, to my surprise,
I found that audiences thought the film slanted in the child's favor. But
one learns to live with misunderstanding. Once the film is finished,
that's all I care about.

s: *Did you ever feel that way as a critic?*
t: I never understood the meaning of a film. I am very concrete.
I only understand what is on the screen. In my whole life, I have never
understood a single symbol.

s: *I would like to talk about* Mississippi Mermaid *for a while. Andrew
Sarris pointed out that the film was cut in New York.*
t: Though the film wasn't very expensive, United Artists considered it
a major project, and because of the stars, they had high hopes for its
success. But the film was a big flop in Paris. The critics didn't like it, nor
did the public—perhaps because Deneuve and Belmondo didn't appear
in their usual sort of roles. Owing to the Paris reception, United Artists
asked me to let them cut about eight minutes out of the film when it
opened in New York. I could have refused, but in this business I hate to
see people losing money on my account. I should have held out,
though, because when the film opened in Japan, it proved a smash: my
greatest success and the greatest success either Deneuve or Belmondo
had ever experienced.

s: *Are you now able to control the cuts producers wish to make?*
t: One never has that power. Frequently, one simply doesn't know
what has been done. For example, I only learned about the cuts in
Stolen Kisses because a journalist who had seen the film in an art house
supported by the government complained that it was shocking to see
cuts in films presented under such auspices. The journalist's article
forced the cinema distributor to replace the scenes. But, of course, that
doesn't always happen, much less get reported.

s: *Many people in the States thought the stars implausible in their roles.*
t: Implausibility is not a crime in all films. *Mississippi Mermaid* is a
fairy tale for adults.

s: *Don't you rather overemphasize that fact—so much so that your serious ideas get compromised? For example, why did you superimpose that colored map of Reunion every time Belmondo took a trip there? I felt the need for more authenticity and fewer tricks to prepare the audience for your final statement about love.*

T: It's possible.

s: *It seemed to me that footage from* Fahrenheit 451 *gets reused when Belmondo has his dream at the clinic.*

T: It seems that way to me, too. Actually, the scene was shot with a monorail in *Fahrenheit*, whereas in *Mermaid* a road of trees were used. It is, you are quite right, the same effect with different means, but I think it works better in *Fahrenheit*.

s: *Why did you include that shot in which Belmondo climbs Deneuve's balcony? It seems to me only an opportunity for Belmondo to show off his athleticism.*

T: Not at all. I did it for myself. First, I set the scene in that square because it is named after Jacques Audiberti, a French writer for whom I have the deepest admiration and whom I always think of when making my films. I wanted it to be very hard for Belmondo to get into Deneuve's room, but also unusual. So I couldn't have him wait for the concierge to leave or somehow steal the key. When I got to the square, I noticed this house with many balconies. First, I had a sign hung, turning it into a hotel (the sign says "Hotel Monorail" because Monorail is the title of one of Audiberti's novels). Then I thought that I would shoot the whole scene of Deneuve leaving the hotel and entering the cabaret and then of Belmondo going to the hotel and climbing from one balcony to the other in one single movement of the camera. That was a fascinating shot. He climbs so I could take it.

A Wild Boy Civilized

DEREK MALCOLM/1970

FRANÇOIS TRUFFAUT was much amused recently when an American critic told him: "Your book on Hitchcock has done you more harm than the worst of your films." He would not have been amused if the critic had said, "Your book on Hitchcock has done him more harm than the worst of his films." He thinks, in fact, that the book—a huge extended interview—succeeded in its primary task of making people revalue upwards the talents of a really great director.

Truffaut is perfectly frank about his adulation of the master upon whose technique, he says, most of his own is based. Yes, he adds, even *The Wild Child*, the film which opened this year's London Film Festival, could not have been made without some of the basic skills learnt from watching Hitchcock movies. Most people, however, see the giant shadow of Renoir, Truffaut's other inspirer, on this humane and marvelously self-effacing story about a doctor's care for a wild boy found in the woods of Aveyron in 1798.

The story, a true one, tells how the doctor (played by Truffaut himself) took the boy away from an institution and into his own home in a long and painstaking attempt to prove that he was capable of becoming more than an animal. Truffaut says that he played the part of the doctor simply because he was able that way to control and shape the performance of Jean-Pierre Cargol as the boy.

He is obviously extremely fond of children and immensely pleased that he has had, since the film opened, a sackful of letters from them

---

From the *Guardian*, 19 November 1970. © Guardian News & Media Limited, 1970. Reprinted by permission.

castigating him for being much too harsh on the wild boy. He says he looks like someone straight out of Dickens when he dons his top hat in the film, and that is perhaps why the kids took against him.

Still, Jean-Pierre himself did not complain when he saw the film as much as he sometimes did when making it . . . particularly when asked to appear naked in the forest scenes. "We had to shoo all the women away from the set or he would not do it. He was very shy, and I sympathized with him. I myself do not like nakedness in films, and there seems to be too much of it. If the body is naked I feel as if I'm watching some kind of medical film. Besides, nakedness is not erotic. It is clothes that make the body sexy."

He found Jean-Pierre Cargol after his assistants and script girls had photographed hundreds of boys coming out of school. There were over 100 screen tests and the choice was eventually made because Cargol not only looked right but was gymnastic enough to manage the tough physical aspects of the part.

Everybody, Truffaut says, asks him what became of the boy (the film ends with his return after running away, thus showing that he is, after all, more human than animal). Well, in fact, the boy lived until he was 40. He had continued under the doctor's care until he was 19, eventually learning to read and write 60 words. Then he lived in a small apartment in Paris under the care of one of the doctor's friends. Not much else had been documented, but since the film had come out, strenuous efforts were being made to find out more.

He agrees that the film, which will probably be shown in this country publicly with Chaplin's *The Circus* was one of his greatest challenges, but he won't say whether he thinks it is also one of his greatest successes. He sees it as a direct descendant of his own *The 400 Blows* and points also to the influence on it of Bresson's *Diary of a Country Priest*. He says he was pleasantly surprised when Hitchcock sent him a telegram of congratulations, which was less ambiguous than usual. Generally, he thinks Truffaut's films rather odd, and once told him that if he had made *Jules et Jim* it would have been a comedy.

Truffaut, now able to make films quite freely, and with few worries about backing, has come a long way since his days as a critic castigating the *ancien regime* in the commercial European cinema. But he has still not lost his taste for seeing other people's movies. He thinks that the really great directors can be excused from worrying about what everybody else is doing. But such an attitude was not for him—"Have you ever heard of an author who does not read books?"

He won't commit himself, though, on fellow members of the old *Nouvelle Vague* except to say that he would never go the way of Godard and that he found his later films progressively more difficult to sit through. There was, however, still a sense of comradeship and admiration. He thinks that he himself will go on making films "in no particular direction except my own" for some years to come.

But he will make no more until 1972. In the next 18 months or so he would edit some new versions of his own scripts and complete André Bazin's unfinished book on Renoir. He would also see a great many films. "You never know," he says, with a modesty he genuinely seems to mean, "I might even improve."

If One Doesn't Like to Hear Talk of Love

YVONNE BABY/1971

FT: Henri-Pierre Roché only wrote two novels. The first, *Jules and Jim*, at 73 years old, and the second at 76. The rest of his work, still secret and unknown, are his diaries (1903–1959). They are very intimate but there appear, under nicknames, celebrated artists, particularly painters: Braque, Picasso, Brancusi, Marcel Duchamp, Marie Laurencin.

Also, in the diaries, to which I had access, I could read the true love story behind *Jules and Jim*—which lasted almost 20 years—and that of the "English girls" whom Roché knew before 1903. Because he took his novels from his diaries, they are already an adaptation from lived experience. So that the screenplay of *Two English Girls* is inspired both by the novel and the diaries.

Roché expressed himself—he said himself—in a manner that was incredibly "airy and tight"—which perhaps comes from his habit of daily writing down his meetings and adventures in a telegraphic style. "After an absence," he noted for example, "I found her again. I took her in my arms. She was my only love from 19 to 23." With a few words, Roché found a very refined form and achieved a happy means of expression which, in my opinion, can be compared with Cocteau. But with added innocence.

I very much approve of the pleasure of manipulating real material. Without losing the idea that the truth is not necessarily credible, nor even interesting, I'm stimulated when I film a story in which the characters really existed. I think of *The Wild Child* and *Two English Girls*. It is often said that the audio-visual will take over little by little from writing.

From *Le Monde*, 25 November 1971. Reprinted by permission of Yvonne Baby.

But I feel that the print medium is more and more attracted to films that unite literature and cinema.

If *Fahrenheit 451* is an homage to all books, the majority of my films are homages to one book. That is why I don't envisage ever doing a traditional adaptation which consists of transforming a novel into a play. If the beauty of a work of literature is in the prose, it is not inconvenient to let the prose be heard in the cinema. For me, the model for this type of adaptation is Bresson's *Diary of a Country Priest*, from Bernanos.

YB: *What are the differences between* Jules and Jim *and* Two English Girls?

FT: The transposition of *Jules and Jim* was easier than that of *Two English Girls*. In the first case, three people live together, in the second, three people are separated and communicate by personal diaries. *Jules and Jim* was filmed from afar, in space and time, and the shock was lessened. For *Two English Girls*, I wanted the audience to feel the emotions of the characters, and if possible to experience them physically. I'm not ashamed to say that I wanted the audience to cry during the film, not only because the actors really cried while playing the roles. And also, because from *The 400 Blows* to now, I've never been afraid of melodramatic situations.

If you don't like to hear talk of love in the cinema, you shouldn't go and see *Two English Girls*. There is not one shot, one sentence that doesn't relate to it. The characters feel very strong sentiments. They're committed to them without a break, and they reach a moment when they are love sick.

For a long time, there has been a lot of talk about the representation of physical love on screen. It appears to me as a normal phenomenon. The cinema has caught up on fifty years of hypocrisy and lies by omission in the field of sexual relations. But it's another thing with *Two English Girls*. Rather than make a film about physical love, I tried to make a physical film about love. Hence the importance of fainting, vomiting, and blood and tears.

YB: *How do you see your characters?*

FT: Claude, the young Frenchman, is Henri-Pierre Roché. What I mean is that he's a man who is defined as a "curious person in the profession." It was he who exhibited the first Picassos in New York before

1910. He had points in common with Proust who, before the striking appearance of *Swann's Way*, was a dilettante surrounded by people who appreciated culture and refinement, but believed himself incapable of becoming an artist.

To understand the two girls, Muriel and Anne, I read a few biographies of the Brontë sisters, and I found enormous similarities. Muriel is a passionate puritan as was Emily. Anne is closer to Charlotte and also fairly close to Catherine in *Jules and Jim*, in the sense that she was a woman before her time. But in the film, I gave Anne the death of Emily Brontë, who, ill for months, refused to see a doctor except two hours before her death.

YB: *Is it a pessimistic film?*
FT: I think it is somber but not pessimistic. If it were, it would have been unfaithful to Roché, in which each line is a testimony to an extraordinary love of life. Generally, most love stories in the cinema are about love thwarted but here the obstacles are almost never exteriorized. They are interior, even mental.

I hope that I haven't seen *Two English Girls* from a masculine angle. Besides, I'm more interested in the femininity of artists than virility, and I hope that in the future there will be more women directors.

YB: *How does the film affect your life?*
FT: At the moment when I think of work, even if you adore it, it must not invade your life, but you must construct a parallel life. For Jean-Pierre Léaud, whom I've watched grow since he was 13, I wanted the film to mark, at the same time, a definite farewell to adolescence, and to Antoine Doinel (*The 400 Blows, Stolen Kisses, Bed and Board*) and his entry into adulthood and into the cinema of others. I wanted to stop seeing him as the character and begin to admire him as an actor.

My profession as a film director has made me very happy. It doesn't exempt me from doubts and I continue to believe in the need for progress even if its lower in comparison to the richness of one's first work. I receive, without much anxiety, the criticisms that are leveled against me, but I take them into consideration where it concerns the execution of the film. But, as it concerns the intentions, I don't think anyone has the right to tell me: "Instead of treating this or that subject you should have been interested in such and such . . ." Nor do I take refuge behind what is called "sacred inspiration" but I have the certitude that the theme of the work invades me completely. For months and sometimes years, before starting the work, I feel that, as the French expression goes: "one tale is good till another is told."

Although it is generally thought that the Doinel series is autobiographical and that the series of adaptations are testimonies to my admiration for literature, the reality is different. I have a great propensity to talk about myself but not directly. For this reason, I have the impression that I am more intimate and sincere through borrowed subjects—*Mississippi Mermaid, The Wild Child*, and *Two English Girls*—than through the Doinel films where I constantly fear the identification between Jean-Pierre Léaud and myself.

I started this film in a bad moral state which was gradually ameliorated during the shoot. What came into my mind was a sentence of Claude's when he has finished his first novel. "I feel better at present. I have the impression that the characters in my book are suffering in my place."

I think that for about 15 years one has ceased, even in Hollywood, to make films in which the story is very spread out in time, films which truly illustrate the notion of time passing. One among them, *The Magnificent Ambersons* by Orson Welles is my favorite. The memory of which I took with me while making *Two English Girls*. Although it happens sometimes that I admire recent films—like *Honeymoon Killers*—my true influences are older. Probably because I need to know by heart and experience annually the works (books, films, music) that have shaken me.

Intensification

GORDON GOW/1972

WHEN HIS FIRST FEATURE-LENGTH FILM, *Les quatre cents coups* in 1959, in spite of its incidental humor, had left audiences deeply concerned about the problem of neglected children, François Truffaut switched to the gag-ridden gangster parody of *Tirez sur le pianiste*. Diversification has been prevalent throughout his career as a director so far. The only firmly consistent thread can be traced in the relatively light-hearted progression of films about Antoine Doinel, the resilient delinquent of *Les 400 coups* whose progression from youth to young manhood has been portrayed over the years by the growing Jean-Pierre Léaud. Otherwise, despite certain inherent resemblances of style, and occasional thematic connections, there has been considerable variety. To follow *Anne and Muriel (Les deux anglaises et le continent)* he has completed quite recently *Une belle fille comme moi*, which he considers to be very close to the freewheeling style he favored so happily in *Tirez sur le pianiste*.

Une belle fille comme moi, based on a Henry Farrell novel, which Columbia had purchased and shelved, has seemed to Truffaut the ideal subject to renew a working association with the witty actress Bernadette Lafont, who was the girl in his early short film *Les Mistons* (1958). The new comedy is said to be both broad and black, concerning a delinquent girl and the showbiz ambitions and numerous love affairs of her past. The cast includes Claude Brasseur as a lawyer and Charles Denner as a rat-catcher. The contrast to the inherently sentimental idealism of *Les deux anglaises et le continent* is a token of Truffaut's avowed preference for contrast. Similarly in 1966 he had chosen the imaginative drama of *Fahrenheit 451*

From *Films & Filming*, 18–22 July 1972.

to follow his 1964 realism of *La peau douce* with its story of a broken marriage and the love of a middle-aged man for a younger girl. Again, in 1969, *L'Enfant sauvage* was a true story to follow the wide-ranging adventures of *La siréne du Mississippi*, from a William Irish novel, in which Jean-Paul Belmondo married his mail-order bride on the remote island where he lived, only to discover that the girl (Catherine Deneuve) was not really the one he had expected: when she vanished the chase led away from the island to the Riviera and the Alps.

With this liking for change, it is hardly surprising that Truffaut should feel that the partly-autobiographical films in which Antoine Doinel has been the central figure should come to a stop now. In any case, he has pointed out, it would be impossible to continue them without turning Antoine into a film director. As it happens, his next film, *La nuit américaine*, is to be about film-making, with Truffaut himself as the director (both in front of the camera and behind it) and Léaud as an actor in the film within the film. This in no way involves the Antoine character (from whom Léaud himself has departed frequently, of course, in other films), but the figure of the director will evidently bear some resemblance to the real Truffaut.

"That's inevitable, certainly. But you will see very little of his personal life. Mostly you will just see him in his professional capacity. The story takes place in a period that begins on the first day of shooting the film within the film, and it ends on the day the shooting is over and the crew separates. The title, incidentally, *La nuit américaine*, is what we say in French for the term *Day-for-Night*, meaning that you shoot night scenes outdoors in the daytime with the use of filters to suggest the appropriate darkness."

It is apt that a Truffaut film should have a title relevant to the technique of cinema, to which he is devoted. His most famous technical effect has been the frozen frame at the end of *Les 400 coups*, when the child at the edge of the ocean gazed back inland, looking towards the apparent emptiness of his future, quizzical, confronting the spectator in the cinema and evoking a deep concern.

"The idea of the frozen frame came to me in the cutting room, moving the film backwards and forwards and stopping and starting; that way you sometimes discover moments that would be lost if you ran them at normal speed. The real reason I used it was that the child didn't play the

scene as I wanted. Jean-Pierre went towards the sea, and he was supposed
to turn and come back, and what I asked him to do was just look at the
camera, to give almost the effect of a stage actor bidding farewell to his
audience, as if he were coming down off the stage and drawing nearer to
the audience. I wanted to be sure the audience would not think he was
going to commit suicide in the water. I needed to establish beyond doubt
that he wasn't going to do that. But when he came up to the camera, he
moved his head around and didn't give that steady look. And then afterwards, while I was editing, I realized that I could get a good effect by
stopping the film earlier. I don't think it's an effect I'd ever seen before;
and indeed I don't think any director has used it previously."

Many have used it since, of course. It has probably been one of the
most emulated single moments in film history, although the frame-
freezing has served all kinds of purposes, comic as well as serious. Truffaut
used it again for a sort of glorification of Jeanne Moreau as Catherine in
Jules et Jim, stopping the action to capture a certain expression and then
resuming normal action speed again. But now he doesn't freeze frames
any more, leaving this useful stylistic device to others, and considering it
to be fair enough that any such effect, once done, becomes common
property, and a part of the vocabulary of cinema: "But naturally I prefer
to see it well used than badly used."

Obviously the critical sense has not forsaken Truffaut, although his
days as a critic of cinema are well behind him. When he started to
direct, he was somewhat apprehensive about his own work being subjected to criticism, the more so because he had been an especially severe
critic himself. "But now I think that a director who has previously been
a critic is inclined to attach less importance to reviews of his work than
other directors might. I don't mean to devalue critics by saying this; but,
having been a critic, one has perhaps more sense of perspective. One by
one, the majority of the films of Orson Welles have been badly reviewed,
and yet his reputation as a film-maker is formidable. The majority of
critics were against most of his films except for *Citizen Kane*, but those
opinions were transitory. I doubt if I would have continued to work as a
critic anyway. Perhaps I'd have written novels or scripts. I've always been
drawn strongly towards literature—towards writing. I made *Fahrenheit
451* because it was about books and their importance: not because it was
science fiction."

Before this, however, there came his attraction to cinema, which he used as a substitute for a satisfactory life between the ages of nine and thirteen. "That was the time when I began to think of myself as a deprived child. I took refuge in the cinema. I stole money to go, or I sneaked in through the exit doors. I had lunch money for school, but I'd skip lunch and school as well to go to the cinema. My parents were never at home, anyway. They liked mountain-climbing and walking through forests. Their attitude to life was rather bohemian." The influence of this upon *Les 400 coups* is not hard to discern; but one might suppose that during those years in real life, the sense of humor might have been less strong in Truffaut than it was at the time he made the first of his Antoine films. For his own part he thinks it was already there. "I remember I laughed quite a lot as a child. I adored Sacha Guitry's films. Once I escaped from home and saw *Le roman d'un tricheur* five times in the one afternoon and evening at a cinema that ran continuously. And whenever I came out of the cinema, even as a child, I'd write down the name of the director. I was very organized about it, and I compiled quite a big file."

Truffaut left school at the age of fourteen. He considers himself to have been a good scholar up to the age of nine, or possibly ten, after which he thinks he was very bad, feeling homeless, and being sent from one place to another to live while his parents were away. "I was completely self-educated at the cinema. For example, the first time I saw Clouzot's *Le Corbeau*, I was quite unfamiliar with a lot of the language in it. They were talking about abortion, injections of morphine, and anonymous letters: things I knew nothing about. But after I'd seen it fourteen times I certainly realized what they meant. It opened up new areas of words for me. One of the reasons I liked that film so much was because all the characters were so disgusting, and this corresponded with my own idea of what society was really like. Whenever I go to see *Le Corbeau* again, those words still stand out in it for me, because that's where I heard them for the first time—and I still love the film. I must have been about eleven when I saw it first.

"After the war years, I began to see American and English films. They were allowed in France again. And the big turning point for me was *Citizen Kane*. Certainly it wasn't typical of American cinema, but it had everything we love about Hollywood combined with everything we love about European cinema. It is an incredibly complete film: the first film made by a young man of twenty-five, and at the same time it's a film which describes a life from beginning to end. I wasn't aware when I saw the picture first that Charles Foster Kane was being put down: I saw him as a marvelous character. Perhaps it was because I was ambitious myself at the time: and I saw the character as a combination of Welles and Kane. Just after I made *Les 400 coups*, there was a re-release of *Citizen Kane* in Paris, and *L'Express* asked me to review it. So I went back to see it; and although I knew it by heart, I understood it then for the first time. I saw then that Welles was against Charles Foster Kane."

It seemed surprising that critics at the time of its original release had not conveyed this to him, but all he recalls of the first Paris reviews of *Citizen Kane* was "the great confusion about the significance of 'Rosebud.' When the film came out, at the point where the sled was burning they hadn't put 'Rosebud' in the subtitles. And most people didn't read the name on the sled. A lot of critics thought 'Rosebud' was the glass paperweight. So, after three weeks of confusion, they put a subtitle in."

Truffaut's declared intention of switching genres from one film to the next can also be found on occasion within a single film. The most extraordinary example of this changing of genre in mid-stream, as it were, is undoubtedly *La sirène du Mississippi* (shown in the USA as *The Mississippi Mermaid* but only seen in Britain for a couple of crowded screenings at the NFT). Graham Petrie in his book *The Cinema of François Truffaut* has written of this director's "desire to dislocate the traditional *genres* especially the detective story, and to make the audiences experience a pattern of emotion totally different to that which they are expecting." This specific film, however, while gripping attention from the very start, is established for nearly three-quarters of an hour in the *genre* of light mystery-thriller, and indeed it retains certain thriller connotations even beyond that period of its running time, the initial lightness serving in my opinion to depreciate the degree of emotional involvement that Truffaut seems to be asking from the spectator during the later phases of the story. The outcome is curious, but never dull—and it warrants consideration among the most interesting of Truffaut's films.

[There follows a lengthy review of *La Sirène du Mississippi* before Gordon Gow returns to the interview.]

As is fairly widely known, Truffaut, like Antoine in his films, spent some time in a reformatory for his petty misdemeanors, and also that he deserted from the army. Now he considers himself fairly moral: "I was never delinquent at heart—I only became delinquent in order to get in to see films." His moral sense, however, can be traced in his own estimation to his benefactor, the editor of *Cahiers du Cinéma* at the time, André Bazin. "He was an exceptionally honest man. It was through him that I really understood what goodness is. It was he who took me out of the reformatory. He promised that he would find me work. Authority for me was taken away from my parents—because an investigation around our district turned out unfavorably for them—and Bazin was made responsible for me. An astounding man. He lived outside Paris, and he'd drive to the Porte de Vincennes in his car, but he considered it shocking for one man to be alone in a car with four seats, and so he would stop at bus stops and pick up people and drop them wherever they wanted to go. When he went to the Cannes Festival, he would loan his car to somebody in Paris, and give his house to somebody else who was in need of accommodation—he was a man like that, who *gave*. He always thought of other people."

Of the Antoine films, the one Truffaut names as the most strictly autobiographical, amusingly enough, is the *Antoine et Colette* sequence of the composite film *L'amour a vingt ans*. "The only difference was that in real life I took the girl to the Cinemathèque, whereas Antoine took her to musical recitals. But the rest was all the same. Moving into a little hotel across the road from where she lived—being invited across all the time, which pleased the parents because it meant that their daughter stayed home—becoming in the girl's eyes like a cousin, just another member of the family, until finally she got bored with me, and went out with another boy while I stayed at home with her parents. Only it didn't happen to me when I was twenty, but when I was eighteen." On the other hand, the mature woman with whom Antoine dallied for a time in *Baisers volés*, and who was delightfully portrayed by Delphine Seyrig, has no basis in fact: "Ah—*malheureusement, non.* She was the realization of the dream of all adolescents—but for me it was only a dream."

The fourth and avowedly the last of these Antoine films was *Domicile Conjugal*, but he is less inclined to see these more personal works as separate from the remainder of his oeuvre than to find a thematic link in such varied subjects as the first Antoine story, *Les 400 coups*, and the Ray Bradbury futuristic sci-fi of *Fahrenheit 451*, and indeed *L'Enfant sauvage* in which he also played a part as the doctor who helped the "wild" child whose early life in a forest had set him apart from the world. "I see each film I make as a kind of mixture of the ones that I made before. But I see those specific three as forming a group. They are about the fundamental things of life. In each of the three there is a handicapped character, a person with disadvantages. Antoine Doinel in *Les 400 coups* lives without the love of his family, which everyone needs. *Fahrenheit 451* is about a man deprived of the culture he could gain from books. And the *enfant sauvage* cannot even speak. For me it seems obviously the main theme, although it is treated in three different ways. The first is autobiographical, the second is through the Bradbury novel, and the third deals with an historical happening."

One of his films which cannot be linked readily to any other (except now, apparently to *Une belle fille comme moi*) is the rip-snorting *Tirez sur le pianiste* (1960). Among its many jests, and its occasional near-subliminal effects, the most famous is the moment where somebody says, "May my mother drop dead if I'm lying," and there is a very rapid cut to an old woman dropping dead within an oval-mask frame. Truffaut looks back on the film with affection.

"I'm very fond of it, but it does remain apart—or has until now—and I think it's because I was very unhappy when I was making it. I found that I didn't like putting gangsters on the screen. It was for that reason that I decided to make it comic. I felt uncomfortable with gangsters, and I had no desire to influence the public to approve of gangsters. That too, is probably because of my childhood, and the way I grew up and everything. And then when I was shooting *Fahrenheit 451* I discovered that I hated filming people in uniform—because, you remember, they were in the fire brigade uniforms, burning the books. So I've decided to have no more uniforms and no more gangsters. Maybe the dislike of uniforms stems from my time in the army.

"Anyway, in *La mariée était en noir* I managed to make a thriller without gangsters and without police." It is in such a film as this, and in certain incidental things like the running gag of the mysterious stranger in *Baisers volés*, that his enthusiasm for Hitchcock finds some thematic expression; but, unlike that other strong Hitchcock admirer, Chabrol, it is not Truffaut's habit to dwell fairly constantly within the thriller genre. "I am more enamored of Hitchcock's way of working than I am of the material that he uses. Every time I see a Hitchcock film I ask myself if I'd have agreed to make a film from such a scenario, and eight out of ten times I think 'No.' The critics look for the Hitchcock influence in anything I make which is within the thriller category, and especially *La mariée était en noir*, of course, but personally I'm more conscious of that influence in something like *L'Enfant sauvage*. That film is primarily a documentary, and the influence Hitchcock's films have had upon me was what enabled me to make it something more than a documentary. And I believe it was understood better, everywhere, than if I had filmed it in a documentary way. What I find in Hitchcock are the answers to two questions: first, how to be understood; and second, how to make it interesting. If you gave the same screenplay to fifty directors from anywhere in the world, Hitchcock would shoot it best.

"There is nothing precise about the outcome of this influence, however, in *L'Enfant sauvage*. There is not one scene in it which resembles anything that Hitchcock has ever done. At the same time, I had the impression that I was helped by what I had gleaned from Hitchcock. What I find absolutely valid in Hitchcock is that he hates documentaries. To feel that way is to see the cinema as better than life: an intensification of life. You can take very small things, very small situations, and make them very interesting. That's what interests me in Hitchcock's work." One is reminded inevitably of the suspense master's oft-quoted maxim: "Drama in life, with the dull bits cut out."

Truffaut in London

CHRIS PETIT AND
VERINA GLAESSNER/1973

FRANÇOIS TRUFFAUT was in London recently for the opening of his latest film *Day for Night* and also to check through the Omnibus documentary that the BBC had prepared on him earlier in the year. "I think he was," confided the press lady, "a little shattered to discover how much of his personal life he exposed on that film."

Q: *Andrew Sarris wrote in his review of* Day for Night *in the* Village Voice *that your film seemed to be made on the premise that there was still an audience who want to be seduced by film. He implied that this audience doesn't exist anymore, that it now wanted to be raped by film. Do you agree?*
A: I don't agree entirely because I think the idea of pleasure is still valid today.

Q: *Do you think there is still a public that wants to approach film in this way?*
A: Yes, I would even say the whole public. For example, a lot of cinema people tell me that they like my film *The Soft Skin* but I know very well that they have only seen it once, whereas *Jules and Jim* they've seen five or six times. This is because they are affected by the idea of pleasure, and they experience more when they see *Jules and Jim*: people who love each other, who live in this beautiful chalet in the country, away from the troubles of society, in the middle of the forest with the little girl. So even

From *Time Out* (London), November 30–December 6, 1973. Reprinted by permission of Chris Petit.

the cinéphiles are moved. I much prefer a film that has charm to one which is made by a technocrat.

Q: *In* Day for Night *you show the cinema to be quite brutal. There's an actor who dies but the main concern of the crew is that the film has to go on. Everything has to be subjected to budgets and deadlines.*
A: That's no contradiction. It's the end result which has to have charm. And anyway, I think the shooting of the film is fairly good-humored, and not at all cruel.

Q: *Well, I find it a bit alarming that an actor is killed and the first thing people think about is how to patch up the film.*
A: But it's the truth. If an actor dies in a plane crash or has a skiing accident, the first thing a director will think about is how he can finish his film.

Q: *I know, but it comes as a kind of shock.*
A: Ah, I knew in doing it that it was a bit shocking. But sometimes a leading actor is forbidden by his contract to travel by plane throughout the shooting, for example. When we are shooting near the mountains, the actors sometimes go skiing on Sundays and I'm sick all day with worry.

Q: *For the actors or for the film?*
A: For the film.

Q: *Why did you play the part of the director?*
A: To make it more real. I thought I was the best person to play the part.

Q: *It's surely a paradox because it isn't a very personal film.*
A: This is because I hide behind all the characters. Sometimes I give a lot of my thoughts to Jean-Pierre Léaud and the other actors. So in *Day for Night* I have a younger representative in Léaud and an older one in Aumont. I have practically no need to say anything. In this film I wanted to show eight characters, because I think the script girl and the prop man are just as important as the director. I answer the question "how does one make a film?" but I have tried to give visual answers the whole time.

Q: *The film within the film looks very bad—one would expect it to be a very bad film.*
A: I think it's like a film of mine, *The Soft Skin*, which was badly received at the Cannes festival.

Q: *Did you see Jacqueline Bisset in any particular film that made you give her the part? Playing a star is a very clichéd thing and yet she's really fresh.*
A: Yes, I saw Stanley Donen's *Two for the Road* several times. I liked her in that. She was only on for ten minutes, in the beginning, when she was starting a love affair with Albert Finney. Then she caught chicken pox and the story continued with Audrey Hepburn. I really thought one could do a version of Audrey Hepburn getting chicken pox and the film continuing with Jacqueline Bisset.

Q: *At the beginning of the New Wave, the French directors were lumped together. Where do you see yourself now in relation to them, both personally and professionally?*
A: I still see a lot of Jacques Rivette and Eric Rohmer. I don't see much of Godard because he is now very much outside the milieu of cinema. Chabrol is always working so we hardly ever see him.

Q: *And professionally? Because you are also a critic and a writer.*
A: I can't really say. I think that everyone has followed his own logical development, but this has underlined the differences rather than the similarities. Each has remained true to himself, but in doing so has drifted away from the others. Have you seen the film about St. Francis of Assisi by Rossellini? Because it's about the same subject, it illustrates what happened to the New Wave. At the end of the film the monks are together and they start to spin around very fast until they fall. When they wake up they all go off in the direction in which they fell.

Q: *About the American cinema. What I thought was very good about* Cahiers *was that it picked up aspects of the American cinema that had previously been ignored. Godard and the gangster movie, yourself and Hitchcock. Do you see anything similar in present American cinema?*
A: I don't think in these terms. I like certain films, I don't like others. That's too general. I've always seen a certain film, a certain director.

I can't answer that. I see them one by one. I think *Day for Night* owes a lot to American films, because I wanted to show people who are working in the same profession; American films do this very well, much better than in Europe. I wanted to do something like the films of Howard Hawks, the ones about flying or hunting. I was also thinking of *Singin' in the Rain* which was a very good film about movie-making—it was very informative as well as making you laugh. That's a great quality.

People who work in the cinema are privileged people, compared to the man in the street or in the audience, so that when things go wrong for them the public doesn't understand. It's difficult to appreciate the problems of someone who is in a privileged situation. I think it's for this reason that I made the film in a light vein. It's a kind of politeness towards the audience. This answers Sarris.

Q: *Can I ask you about* Such a Gorgeous Kid Like Me? *I really liked it, although I think I'm about the only person who did.*
A: Yes, you are.

Q: *Are you satisfied with the film?*
A: I can't be satisfied because when one makes a comedy it should make the audience laugh.

Q: *I laughed.*
A: You see *Two English Girls* was a very black film, without any humor, and if people didn't like it I said to myself, "They don't like it, never mind. I needed to make that film." But I can't be happy with *Such a Gorgeous Kid Like Me* because if people didn't find it funny there must be something wrong.

Q: *Was it just the critics who didn't find it funny, or was it the public as well?*
A: The public was embarrassed as well, they weren't happy. I think I know where the mistake was: the film was too much about the boy and not enough about the girl. I'm on the girl's side, but I filmed the boy with lots of realism, and a lot of people identified with him, with the sociologist. They're very unhappy because things go badly for him and they think the girl is unpleasant, so they can't sympathize with her.

That was the mistake, I think. I ought to have had a very strong actor to play the sociologist. I should have created a character who was not so weak, but the actor should have been stronger.

Q: *Were you influenced by Nelly Kaplan's film at all, because it's a very similar character out to get revenge?*
A: No, when I read the book I thought of Bernadette Lafont. It was after *Two English Girls*, which was a rather sick film, a little unhealthy, a little morbid. Too sad, too slow. So I needed to do something completely different, to take everything in hand again. *Such a Gorgeous Kid Like Me* was in a way an experience of vitality because I found it necessary to go in the opposite direction to *Two English Girls*. It had been too weak, not enough tension, I wanted to do something frantic and I think the two films are exaggerated, each in its own direction. *Two English Girls* is too gloomy, without enough vitality, and the other is too nervous. *Day for Night* is in some ways the reconciliation because there are sad scenes and happy scenes. The mixture works well. I'm made to do films which contain both elements.

Q: *I felt about the film that it was taking the character of Catherine from* Jules and Jim, *making her destructiveness more overt, more positive.*
A: I don't know. It's the same character in *The Bride Wore Black* as well. For me, Bernadette Lafont is the female version of *The Wild Child*, a sort of wild child. It's for this reason that I choose very different subjects, to hide the same things. Because I know they're always the same.

Q: *Do you tend to make the same films?*
A: Yes, more or less.

Q: *Would you ever contemplate making another film in English, like* Fahrenheit 451?
A: I don't know.

Q: *How did you manage to make a film in English?*
A: It was no problem for me. It's usual to change a lot of the dialogue and the scenario, and of course I couldn't make any changes. But there were advantages, it was all very professional. I think it's the most

professional of all my films because of the organization and because of
the people I was working with. The sound and the pictures are excellent
too—visually it's a very strong film—but it's a film without any characters. The story is too important and the characters aren't quite right,
not human enough. I don't quite know what to make of it. When one
sees clips from all the films, it's always the clips from *Fahrenheit* which
are the best. They make people want to see the film. But I'm not sure
about the film as a whole.

Q: *What are you working on at the moment?*
A: Books, books about movies, Bazin and myself. And some screenplays.

Q: *Have you any plans to make a film?*
A: No.

Q: *You're not giving up the cinema, I hope?*
A: Oh no. Just for two years, a year and a half.

Adèle H

GILBERT ADAIR / 1975

EVEN IF UNAWARE that it housed the offices of *Les Films du Carrosse*, François Truffaut's production company, one would be drawn to make a comparison between the rue Robert Estienne, a modestly picturesque cul-de-sac off the Champs Elysees, and some studio set: memories of Clair, Becker, perhaps even the matching courtyards of Renoir's *Le Crime de Monsieur Lange* and Truffaut's own *Domicile Conjugale*. On one wall of the office itself is an enlarged *Peanuts* strip (Linus tearing out his hair as Lucie reveals the meaning of Rosebud); on another, in poster form, the headline "Kane Found With Singer in Love-Nest."

When I spoke to him, Truffaut had just finished editing his fourteenth feature, *L'Histoire d'Adèle H.*, written, as almost always, with Jean Gruault and the indispensable Suzanne Schiffman. Adèle, played by Isabelle Adjani, was Victor Hugo's youngest daughter, who shared her father's exile in the Channel Islands until she met, at one of the table-turning séances organized by the poet, a young English lieutenant, Albert Pinson, and fell in love with him. One can no longer know for certain whether or not they were engaged to be married; in Adèle's mind there was no doubt, but the Englishman would appear to have treated the affair as a passing flirtation and soon departed with his regiment to Halifax in Nova Scotia. Whereupon Adèle herself upped and left, following the man she considered her fiancé halfway across the Empire but never conclusively tracking him down.

Should the initial H suggest a case-history? I asked Truffaut. "Not really. Adèle was the less loved of Hugo's two daughters—the favorite,

From *Sight and Sound*, Summer 1975. Reprinted by permission of *Sight and Sound*.

Léopoldine, drowned with her husband in 1843—and often traveled incognito. She was, you understand, the daughter of the most famous man in the world, a fact of which she was proud but which must have occasioned a certain suffering. Perhaps this might better explain her desire (or should I say *idée fixe*), to conceal her identity, to exchange the too famous name of Hugo, which was not hers but her father's, for another. And identity, I suppose, is the real subject of the film.

"If, as I'm sometimes reproached, my films are in contradiction with the age I live in, it's perhaps in the sympathy I continue to feel for anyone who must struggle to gain entry to a society from which he was excluded at the outset. This is the theme of the Antoine Doinel films. It's also the theme of *L'Enfant Sauvage*, which I made at a time when many young people, hardly older than the child in my film, were throwing off their culture, and their clothes, and practically going to live in the forest! If *L'Enfant Sauvage* depicted a creature desirous of acquiring an identity—and that he *desired* it, I truly believe—Adèle's concern is to lose one which she can never consider her own."

Oddly enough, it was in 1969, while shooting *L'Enfant Sauvage*, that Truffaut came across Adèle's diaries, which had been decoded and edited by an American, Frances Vernor Guille. The earlier film, too, was based on a journal, which gave it a kind of rigor unusual in his work but shared, he feels, by *Adèle*. "Though I've also tried to give it something of the intensity of *Les Deux Anglaises et le Continent*."

Truffaut spoke of the extent to which he is willing to "remake" his works. "If a film has failed to satisfy either the public or myself, I have a fantasy about starting it all over again. Which is impossible, of course, but I do attempt to avoid the same mistakes in any later film dealing with a similar emotional situation. If, for example, the public refused to accept the character played by Jean Desailly in *La Peau Douce*, it was doubtless because when I adopt the point of view of a male character I have a tendency to make him—not exactly weak, but like a child. So, in *Domicile Conjugal*, where I re-employed certain themes of *La Peau Douce*, it was from a more frankly comic angle and with an actor, Jean Pierre Léaud, whom the public has never ceased to consider as a child. Likewise, in *L'Enfant Sauvage*, I now believe I was wrong not to disclose what finally happened to the child, and you'll see at the end of *Adèle*

I've used a montage of photographs and documentation so that no one will be left in ignorance of her fate."

For Isabelle Adjani, a young actress who became a pensionnaire of the Comédie-Française at the rather unlikely age of 17, Adèle Hugo is a first major film role. "What excited me most," said Truffaut, "was working with an actress who is still evolving, still developing. It was exactly the same with Léaud, which is, incidentally, why there can be no further chapter in the Doinel series." In a few weeks, however, Truffaut is planning to shoot a film whose cast will consist almost entirely of children between the ages of six months and twelve years, *L'Argent de Poche*. "I intend it to have a much more controlled narrative line than would be possible with a mere collection of sketches, but still be free enough to let me improvise as much as I can. Otherwise, what is the point of filming children? You see, everything a child does in a film, it's as if he were doing it for the first time. So it's as precious as a home movie."

I asked him finally what sort of reaction to, say, *L'Histoire d'Adèle* would please him most. "I don't really want to make an audience cry. In a way, that's too easy. Perhaps I'd prefer that they *tremble*—yes, that's it, tremble." How would he feel then, if some manager felt obliged to place a sign outside his cinema, declining any responsibility for shock caused by the film? Truffaut laughed. "Oh, you can't know how proud I'd be!"

Isabelle A Plays Adèle H

PATRICK THEVENON / 1975

TEN WEEKS IN GUERNSEY to shoot *The Story of Adèle H*, who was the youngest daughter of Victor Hugo. One imagines the poet, playwright, and novelist's exile here at Hauteville House. Adèle kept a diary of the actions and conduct, sayings and doings of the great man who, above on the terrace, wrote *La Legende des siécles*, standing facing the sea while below his mistress, Juliette Drouet, collected fresh eggs which she brought to him punctually every morning.

As for Victor Hugo, the film shows not even his shadow, nor any other member of his family except Adèle. "Putting great men on screen, that's the way of television," says François Truffaut, whose precedent film, *Day for Night*, has just won an Oscar.

Unusually, the film tells a love story of one character. In 1854, Adèle Hugo—played here by Isabelle Adjani—("Isabelle A" as Truffaut refers to her)—beautiful, intelligent, courted—falls in love with a certain lieutenant Albert Pinson (played by Bruce Robinson), a vain Englishman who turned up at the Hugos', probably interested in a dowry. What happened between Adèle and Albert? Not much, it seems. Nevertheless, sufficient for the young woman to spend the following 18 years pursuing him. Crossing oceans in the wake of his regiment, living alone in miserable lodgings, meeting her loved one for two minutes every six months, by accident in the street, enduring rebuffs, giving him a great part of the sums of money that were sent to her by her family, never discouraged by anything, even by the marriage of Albert. And keeping, hour after hour, the diary of her passion written in a code still undeciphered if not undecipherable.

From *L'Express*, 3–9 March 1975. Reprinted by permission of *L'Express*.

Finally, in 1872, Victor Hugo obtained the right to get Adèle repatriated from Barbados thanks to a black slave that had seduced her—"The first negro in my life"—the septuagenarian poet noted in his diary—and got his daughter admitted into a sanitarium. Adèle died aged 85 in 1915.

"She lived this passion 100%," according to Truffaut, "but it remained a family secret for a long time." It was a very knowledgeable American woman, Frances Vernor Guille, who rediscovered her trace and consulted the correspondence between Victor Hugo in Guernsey, his wife in Brussels, his sons François and Charles, in Paris. The book published by Mrs. Guille (*Letters of the family, Diary of Adèle for the year 1852*) has fascinated Truffaut for 6 years, and he wrote six screenplays before deciding to film it.

What prompted him to action was Isabelle A arrived. When Adèle H meets her lieutenant Pinson, she is 24 years old. When she crosses the ocean to rejoin him (the moment at the beginning of the film), she is 33. When she returns to France (the end of the film) she is 42. Isabelle A is 19. This rupture between the subject and the interpreter, François Truffaut justifies like this: "I was looking for an actress who spoke English perfectly, because the film (Budget: 4,500,000 Francs) was shot simultaneously in two versions. Someone told me to see *La Gifle* (*The Slap*), in which Isabelle Adjani plays scenes in English. "I went and voilà!"

Faced with the incredulity that this trivial motive provoked, he responds to no questions on Isabelle Adjani, and doesn't say why he doesn't respond to any questions about Isabelle Adjani. On reflection, he agreed to write about her himself. (See separate article.) Perhaps to prevent others from spoiling his miracle with their words.

For Isabelle Adjani is a miracle and, if François Truffaut filmed *The Story of Adèle H*, it's the story of Isabelle A. that we hear him telling. Was it she that pushed him to write the sixth version of the script in three days? "I wanted to make the film with her urgently," he writes, and "it's necessary to shoot every day, even Sunday."

The miracle is that she is a happy, young healthy girl, who likes her food, and has strong ideas which she expresses beautifully. She considers that she's never done anything until now, and that Adèle H. is perhaps her first role. She understands that she is seductive, because, successively, in two years she seduced Nina Companeez (*Faustine*), Raymond Rouleau (*School For Wives* and *Ondine*), Robert Hossein (*The House of Bernarda Alba*),

Jean-Paul Roussilon (*The School for Wives* again), Claude Pinoteau (*The Slap*) without forgetting Pierre Dux (who engaged her for the Comedie-Française).

A for all, and all for A. But such a quick and massive success seems to her inexplicable. But at the same time, she reacts against the idea of luck or accident. When she reads something about "the fairy tale of Isabelle Adjani," she sees red. "I'm not the Little Match Girl".

With this conscience about her value and the astonishment that success has brought her comes a feeling of insecurity which doesn't always help her work. "Everything went very well," says Truffaut. "But we had some harmonious disagreements," adds Isabelle Adjani.

To raise herself in her own eyes, she expects to always give more. Much more than her director demands. "I think any other actress could do as well. However, I know that if the camera creates 60% of the emotion then I must create 60% too in my performance. Also if it is 20% too much, it will be bad."

With a certain malaise, Isabelle Adjani refuses to see the rushes. She fears to find a gap between them and what she expects. And Truffaut avoids rehearsing her. They shoot immediately, before she feels she has attained what she wanted. *The Story* of *Adèle H* is a film on passion, but unrequited passion.

After the shoot, François Truffaut will gain the solitude of the editing room, and Isabelle Adjani will have an embarrassment of choices. Hollywood has already left its card. This second step will be easier for her.

"I've done my novitiate. And now they ask me to enter orders. I was seized by fear. I didn't know what decision to make. I hesitated for two months. How could I have kept François Truffaut waiting two months?"

She is Isabelle A, and what she means to Truffaut, he will let nobody else say.

Kid Stuff

JOSEPH McBRIDE AND
TODD McCARTHY/1976

FRANÇOIS TRUFFAUT'S LATEST FILM, *L'Argent de Poche*
(*Small Change* in the U.S.) opened in France last spring to the best
response he has had from the public since his first feature *The 400 Blows*.
The fact that both films deal with childhood is no coincidence. Truffaut
has an uncanny gift for directing children, an empathy, a delicacy, a
charm unmatched by any other director working today. Before shooting
Small Change, an episodic film with 200 children in the cast, Truffaut told
us he was worried that adults would find it too childish, because it was
"full of kids' jokes." As it happens, the films' greatest strength is Truffaut's
ability to get into the minds of his young cast members and express their
feelings without condescension. To use Jean-Luc Godard's characterization of Truffaut, *Small Change* is both "rigorous and tender" in its
approach to growing up.

After playing the New York Film Festival, *Small Change* will be
released here by Roger Corman's New World pictures, which handled
the successful U.S. release of Truffaut's previous film, *The Story of Adele
H.* New World could not use the literal translation of the new film's
title, *Pocket Money*, because it was used in 1972 for a film starring Paul
Newman and Lee Marvin.

Most of Truffaut's time in the last few months has been spent on location for Steven Spielberg's *Close Encounters of the Third Kind*, a science-
fiction movie in which he plays a French UFO expert. It is the first time

Truffaut has acted for another director since he was an extra in René Clement's *Le Chateau de Verre* (1950), and he has mixed feelings about the experience. He admires Spielberg and finds it interesting to study American production methods (one of the reasons he accepted the role), but the long waits between set-ups in Mobile, Alabama, have taken their toll on Truffaut's patience.

To help pass the time, he has been writing a book, *L'attente des acteurs*, roughly translated as *Actors' Waiting*, a title inspired by the title of Ingmar Bergman's film *Women's Waiting*. He has also been working with Suzanne Schiffman on the screenplay of his next film, *The Man Who Loved Women*, which he plans to shoot in France this fall (assuming *Close Encounters* is finished) with Charles Denner in the title role. We interviewed Truffaut in his suite at the Beverly Hills Hotel, where he writes in a cloud of cigar smoke, under a photograph of Ernst Lubitsch. When Truffaut visits Los Angeles, as he has done frequently in the last year, his purpose is three-fold: to stock up on Montecristo cigars at Dunhill's, to read the film books he buys at Larry Edmonds' book shop, and to visit Jean Renoir. Truffaut showed *Small Change* to Renoir in June (Renoir told us he was "moved to tears" by the film) and our interview took place a few days later. It was conducted in both French and English.

Q: *In your introduction to the screenplays of the four Antoine Doinel films, you said that the first one,* The 400 Blows, *was originally conceived as a sketch in an omnibus film about children.* Small Change *could have been that film.*
A: Exactly. I had that project in mind before *The 400 Blows*, when I did *Les Mistons*. Originally, I had five or six stories about children. I started with *Les Mistons* because it was the least expensive: no interior scenes, no problem with lighting, all I needed was the film and the people. But I felt *Les Mistons* was too literary: the story couldn't have been told without the narration. After that, I wanted to keep working with children, but I wanted to do things which were more correct. *The 400 Blows* started with a scene that finally wound up in the middle of the film; it just grew out and became an entire film. The germ of the idea was the boy who didn't go to school for three days in a row, and had to come back with an excuse; he said his mother was dead, and he spent the night outdoors. I felt I had to explain what came after that and what came before.

Q: *The new film has such a large cast, and involves so many incidents—*
how did you and Suzanne Schiffman approach the screenplay?
A: Initially, I had a few stories; six, maybe seven. For instance, the little girl who shouts "I'm hungry" through the window [using a bullhorn
after her parents lock her in the apartment] was a story someone had
told me. Another, "I go boom" [a baby miraculously survives after
falling from a window], was from a newspaper. The job with Suzanne,
was to bring all the stories together. We repeated the principle for *Day*
For Night. Each time something got complicated, we'd say, "Unity of
place: a small town. Unity of time: two months before vacation." Since
there wasn't a unity of action, having the other two unities helped us.
French literature professors make a big deal of the three unities in the
theater of Jean Racine. It's a very French obsession; it can help you
when you work. When you adapt a book, you can cut out the pages
you don't like, but when you're starting with a blank page, you have to
create your own discipline. If you just throw all these stories into the
unified framework of the town, then it'll take shape. It's important that,
if one child is to become more significant than the others, you meet
him at the beginning of the film: you can't just haphazardly meet a lot
of kids as you go along. It has to be established.

Q: *There were some characters you brought in and then dropped, such as*
Little Gregory, the one who falls out of the window. He was never seen again.
A: Actually he was seen one more time, in the nursery. But it was
very difficult to shoot with him. *Very* difficult. I was afraid that at any
moment his mother would come in and say "That's it."

Q: *Did you have lots of mothers on the set?*
A: Just this one. We had to take care of the children ourselves. Suzanne
took some and I took some. We had responsibility over them, so their
mothers didn't have to be there. We did have a nurse on the set—she's
the one in the film who runs through the schoolyard after the medical
examination. She was actually a nurse for all the children.

Q: *It seems there are two strains of thought in* Small Change. *There is the*
character played by Gregory Desmouceaux, whose story is like Stolen Kisses*:*
he gives flowers to an older woman, falls in love with a young girl. Then there

is Philippe Goldman, whose story is like The 400 Blows: *he's a delinquent whose family abuses him. It's almost as if you have two protagonists.*
A: The dark side and the optimistic side.

Q: *The dark side is dropped in favor of the optimistic side, because Goldman leaves the film and the story ends with Desmouceaux's first kiss. Did you want to stress the optimistic side of childhood?*
A: Certainly it's stronger in the film. Probably because I'm growing older quickly. I believe that in directing *The 400 Blows* I was Antoine Doinel's brother, in *The Wild Child*, I was Victor's father, now, I'm a grandfather. But I suppose the real reason is that, more than the others, *Small Change* was done in collaboration with children. They would come around, gather at the editing table, talk together. They saw the rushes. And because there were a lot of little children—almost all of them were pre-adolescent—it more and more became a film *for* them. And that's what makes it less sad. When I was in the middle of shooting the scene of the boy stealing the ornament off the car, the children saw it in the editing room and they were very upset. They said, "Now the person who owns the car will know who stole it, and he'll get mad." I always had problems like that. And to satisfy the children I made the film less cruel.

Q: *You wanted to tell it from the child's point of view?*
A: Yes, when you tell a story to a child, they always want to find optimistic happy things in it. When my daughters were little, I told them stories that had both elements. For example, I told one story about a little girl who spent the night in a bakery. She had a problem—being locked up—but she also had the fun of being able to eat lots of cake. At the end of the story, I would put in an element of Hitchcock's *Marnie*. I told them how the girl got out of the bakery: she waited until morning, when the scrubwoman came to clean the floor. [In *Marnie*, Tippi Hedren avoids capture while burglarizing an office because the scrubwoman is deaf.] The other reason for the optimism in *Small Change* is because I had just done *Adele H.*, so the shooting was very oppressive; it was hard being on that island all the time. Because of that, *Small Change* was a liberation. I always make a film that's contrary in mood to the film that came before it.

Q: *The mis-en-scéne is very simple in* Small Change, *apparently because you couldn't have complicated shots for the children.*

A: It had to be because children can't be concerned with the camera. In the classroom scenes, I told them to forget the camera, because they were supposed to be paying attention to the teacher. If I had tried to do tracking shots in the class, for example, it would have been impossible. Also, it's very tiring for children to work eight hours a day. You have to let them get out and have fun while you're setting up, then when you're ready, they come back and go into it right away. Quite often there was only one take.

Q: *Allan Dwan said that when he was directing Shirley Temple, he made it a game for her, yet George Cukor after directing* The Blue Bird *said you can't make it a game with children, because it's such hard work. Do you agree with Dwan or with Cukor?*

A: It depends on the age of the children. Because they're five years old, they don't know that it's work. You have to use ruses and games. Give them gum, whatever, it doesn't matter. But after they're five, they know it's work and they know they're collaborating with you in creating something.

Q: *How old was Sylvie Grezel, the girl who said "I'm hungry" through the bullhorn?*

A: Seven-and-a-half. She was a true collaborator on the film. I would tell her what to do, and she would say, "I'll do it if nobody else is around." When she said "I'm hungry" she didn't want anyone else around her. She would tell me before every scene if she was in agreement with me or not. But with little Gregory, who was two-and-a-half, it was very rough. He hated staircases and he hated the woman [Nicole Felix] who played his mother. He knew that she had to talk like she was his mother, and he didn't want to play that game. When he found out that he had to wear the same clothes every day, he started to tear them off.

Did you notice the little Vietnamese girl in the film? She was the daughter of the make-up woman on the film [Thi-Loan N'Guyen] who played the woman who was hypnotized in *Adele H.* And on *Small Change*, she brought her little daughter, Tu. She was a very intelligent girl; I treated her like my assistant. Especially with Gregory. The little girl stood next to me, and when I touched her on the head, she would say "*Moteur*! Action! Cut!" Little Gregory found it amusing to obey her. If I had to do a traveling shot, I would touch her on the shoulders, she would move along with me, and Gregory would move along very naturally. It worked like chewing gum. But he's the most difficult actor I've worked with since Oskar Werner!

Q: *Gregory did some of the most marvelous things in the film, such as the scene where he's sitting on the floor throwing food around.*
A: [Sighs] Ah, yes. That took half an hour.

Q: *How did you shoot the scene of Gregory falling out of the window?*
A: We used two identical kitchens, one on the first floor of the apartment house and the other eight or nine stories high. When we did the shots from the ground, it was a doll that somebody was moving. Very effective.

Q: *When I watched the scene, I felt sure the baby wouldn't die because I remembered that you once said a director doesn't have the right to show a child dying in a film.*
A: I didn't say that. I said that a director has a responsibility with that kind of scene. You should do it only if it's very important; you must have very good reasons. In Rossellini's film *Germany, Year Zero* there was a child who committed suicide. It was a very good film.

Q: *And the same is true of Bresson's* Mouchette. *What are some other films about childhood you admire?*
A: *Zero de Conduite, The Innocents, Village of the Damned,* and two films by Luigi Comencini, *Icompreso* and *Pinocchio*.

Q: *What do you think of Leo McCarey's films with children?*
A: Oh, they're very good.

Q: *Especially the Nativity scene in* The Bells of St. Mary's.
A: I haven't seen it. When I was young, I didn't want to see it because it was about nuns and priests. I was terrified! I still am! But now I'd like

to see the film. When I was young I didn't want to see pirate films. Never. Westerns—I didn't like horses. I didn't like nuns and priests.

Q: *How many of the children in* Small Change *did you know before making the film? Gregory Desmouceaux?*
A: I've known him since he was born. His mother used to be my secretary. The other one, Philippe Goldman, who plays the battered child, I didn't know until I made the film. He came to the auditions, and I found that he resembled the portraits of the young Napoleon at the time of his first victory. Others such as Sylvie Grezel, I knew for several years. She's a little girl who never talks to anybody. But, she would always let me take her picture, so every year I would take one of her during her summer vacation. Most of the children in the film came from the village of Thiers.

Q: *Was this the first film for all the children?*
A: Oh, yes.

Q: *You wouldn't use professional child actors?*
A: I don't know. There aren't any in France—maybe in commercials. I don't have any theory about child actors.

Q: *Would you like to make a film with Tatum O'Neal?*
A: I like her very much, but there's the problem of communication. It's not possible.

Q: *Were the audition methods the same as you used for* The 400 Blows?
A: The same. 16 mm. "What is your name? Do you like movies?" When I shot the tests for *The 400 Blows*, one little boy came and I asked him, "Which was the last film you saw?", and he said, "*The Seventh Seal* by Ingmar Bergman," and he told me the whole story. He was one of the kids in the classroom: now he's a good TV director.

Q: *What's become of some of the other kids you've directed—such as Fido in* Shoot the Piano Player *or René, Jean-Pierre Léaud's friend in* The 400 Blows?
A: The one in *400 Blows* [Patrick Auffray], he became more interested in politics and dropped acting because the light hurts his eyes too much. He joined the Young Gaullists.

Q: *And Fido—Richard Kanayan?*
A: He tried to do music-hall singing, but he wasn't very original, he could only imitate Aznavour. So he became a tailor.

Q: *And* The Wild Child, *Jean-Pierre Cargol?*
A: He just married, three months ago. [Truffaut laughs heartily, as if he can't believe it.] A whole group lives with his uncle, a very famous guitarist, Manitas de Plata. I don't know if he's really good, but everybody likes him. The snobs like him very much—Picasso signed his guitar. Very strange.

Q: *What about the little girl in* Jules and Jim, *Sabine Haudepin?*
A: She's an actress. Her brother was Jeanne Moreau's son in *Moderato Cantabile.* Both of them are still acting, they're about twenty now.

Q: *Would you want to make another Antoine Doinel film?*
A: I don't know. I don't know. Maybe.

Q: *Did you consider using Léaud in* Small Change *to play the father of one of the kids?*
A: Oh, no, because *The 400 Blows* is a very Parisian film, and *Small Change* is about the provinces. It isn't the same world.

Q: *Yet, you appeared in it, playing the girl's father in the opening scene.*
A: Yes, but that was a last-minute decision. The shooting was finished, and we were on our way back to Paris, when we saw a monument reading "The Center of France." And I put it in the film. I cut myself into the scene just to make it shorter.

Q: *It seemed metaphorical to have that shot at the beginning: the center of France. You mean to imply, evidently, that the children in the film are representatives of French society at that age.*
A: I've got the same idea for America. Here, there's an opposition between the East Coast and the West Coast. People in New York speak badly of California people, and California people don't like New York people. I always thought I'd like to do something to reconcile these opposite points of view. If I were President of the United States, I would

determine the exact center of the United States and I would build a huge park, bigger than Disneyland, and make everybody come there. And that would be very useful, no? I have a great passion for Brasilia. I think, it's a great idea, because it's sad in Brazil: you have all the people in Rio, and then this huge open country. Building Brasilia was a magnificent idea. But perhaps it wasn't a success.

Q: *In a sense* Small Change *reminded me of* The 400 Blows, *in that the school resembled a military institution. The teachers wore uniforms and it seemed regimented. Even the summer camp seemed military.*
A: I don't know. Maybe it's a little more so than in America. But there wasn't any special point; that's just the way it is. When you have the responsibility of a hundred kids in summer camp, you need some sort of discipline.

Q: *The difference between the two schools in the two films is that in* Small Change *the teachers are more sympathetic.*
A: Yes, absolutely. Because the teachers are changing. They're younger. They're more liberal, politically, than they used to be. It's not so oppressive. There's a much better relationship between the kids and the teachers today than there was then. But the teachers are still a bit demagogic. The character played by Jean-François Stevenin is a little demagogic; he wants to be friends with the kids. The female teacher [Chantal Mercier] is more honest. She's tougher. She's like that; she was a supervisor in a girls' school for seven years. The teacher in *The 400 Blows* was very real to me. He's what I had known in school. But it's becoming rarer to have a teacher like that, because the teachers today read *La Nouvelle Observateur*.

Q: *Was Stevenin meant to be taken as you?*
A: His ideas, yes. They're my ideas. In France, a lot of people criticized the speech he makes to the kids. They liked the movie but they didn't like the speech. But they never made very intelligent criticisms of it. I think it's the truth, line by line. The leftists think it's too conciliatory. The people on the right think it's too left-wing. I thought it was a necessary scene, to have those thoughts expressed.

Q: *Your daughters, Laura and Eva, both appear in* Small Change. *Laura was born in 1959, the year you did* The 400 Blows. *So her life exactly spans the period between the two films. Now that you've had the experience of fatherhood all those years, it must give you a different perspective on childhood.*

A: It forced me to, yes. In many ways. But I can't say how.

Q: *Perhaps it's that being a father makes one more tolerant of one's own parents mistakes.*

A: That's exactly how it is for me. Because I am divorced, and I feel some culpability as a result. I think *The 400 Blows* is a very cruel film towards adults. But in *Small Change* I show the adults with a little more—what is the word?—resignation. They've lost something of their responsibility, the adults in *Small Change*. They do have weaknesses.

Q: *In the film you deal more with boys than with girls.*

A: Ah, it's true. Yes. Maybe someday I'll do a film about a fourteen-year-old girl. It's an old project of mine.

Q: *People say in America that because discipline in the schools is not as strong as it once was, the students aren't learning as much.*

A: In France, the level of education is falling all the time.

Q: *What's the solution? Not more discipline?*

A: No, no. The main problem is that too many people become teachers for the wrong reasons. And it's probably the most important profession in the world. A lot of people have become teachers because they're weak but they want to find a strong role in life. They're afraid to enter adult life, so they become teachers. Often, they prolong their studies to exaggerated lengths because they're afraid of the competitive aspects of real life. Becoming a teacher is yet another prolongation of this student life. All this is very bad, because children shouldn't be educated by someone who is weak. One should have a vocation for being a teacher. One should want to teach, want to get something across to the students.

Q: *Stevenin's motive for being a teacher in* Small Change *is admirable: he had had a bad childhood, so he wanted to make up for it by helping his students. It reminded me of the girl in* Day for Night *saying to Léaud, "You should stop blaming other people for your unhappy childhood and start to grow up."*

A: Yes, very funny line. In *Bed and Board*, Claude Jade criticized the book that Doinel was writing about his parents, because it was a form of revenge. She said, "You should never take this kind of revenge." I believe that.

Q: *What do you think will become of Goldman's character in* Small Change? *Do you think he'll come through his ordeal all right?*
A: Oh, not too good.

Q: *Stevenin expresses the hope that he will.*
A: He may be better off than he was, but I don't think it will go too well for him. He'll be in a public institution. There are problems in places like that as well. The children are unhappy there because they don't have enough money and there aren't any comforts. Recently, in one of these orphan asylums, there wasn't much money, and someone discovered that the pharmaceutical manufacturers were experimenting on them, changing their hair color, trying out new creams and ointments. The drug company gave money to the director of the institution to do these tests on kids. It's incredible, isn't it? It was a little scandal that people talked about for a while and then forgot.

Q: *You never showed Goldman actually being beaten.*
A: Oh, impossible, impossible!

Q: *There was a scene like that in Chabrol's* A Rupture.
A: I didn't like it. You could do it in silent pictures—for instance, *Broken Blossoms*—because without sound there was a stylization. With color and sound, it's impossible.

Q: *By not showing it, you avoided melodrama.*
A: Yes, I never show things like that. I never show anything which would make you sick to your stomach. One is responsible for what one shows. It's enough just to suggest it.

Q: *It would seem that* Small Change *is your ultimate film about childhood up to this point.*

A: Yes, because it has what you could call a global point of view.

Q: *Yet one has the impression that it isn't your last word on the subject.*
A: No. When I go back to the subject, it will be easier to make a film
that deals with only one child. When I made *The Wild Child*, I was a bit
anxious in shooting the scenes at the Institute with all the other children around, because it was really the story of one child, and the others
were so good. It was then that I decided to do a film with a lot of children, and to do a film with improvisation. That's why I started *Small
Change* by showing the kids at school, so you can see all of them. Now I
can go back to the story of a single child.

Q: *It's unlikely that* Small Change *could have been made in America—
unless you had Tatum O'Neal.*
A: It's true. In France, you can do a film without stars. It's a little harder,
maybe, to find the money, but once it's made, it's distributed as well as a
film with Belmondo or Alain Delon. There's no discrimination.

Q: *In America, films aren't treated equally.*
A: Because they begin by saying, "This is a B-movie." That's one of the
reasons why I'd be worried about making a film here. I like to make
films which start with a small premise. It's very hard to do that here.
When I look back at the last twenty years of American films, the ones I
like are those which are completely off in the margins, such as *Johnny
Got His Gun* and *The Honeymoon Killers*. But in France they consider me
a very traditional filmmaker. I don't know if it's true.

Q: *Alain Resnais once said that each film should be capable of being summed
up in a single sentence. Would you agree with that, and if so, what would be the
sentence to sum up* Small Change?
A: It's the idea that kids are thick-skinned.

François T

L'EXPRESS: *Steven Spielberg made contact with you for you to take the role of Professor Lacombe, in* Close Encounters of the Third Kind. *How did it come about?*

FRANÇOIS TRUFFAUT: He called me through a common friend in February 1976. I was busy completing the cutting of *Small Change*. I thought at first that it was a misunderstanding. I'm unable to speak English and I couldn't imagine that the role was in French. Steven sent me the script and I read it rapidly without understanding it very well. It was very technical. We spoke on the telephone. I explained to him that I wasn't an actor, that I could only play myself as in *Day For Night*. Finally, I accepted. There are only five scenes in which I appear. I got the impression that it wouldn't take up too much of my time.

L'EXPRESS: *For the first time you were in a film that was not your own. Did you feel like a spectator?*

F. TRUFFAUT: From the start, I felt like an actor. I felt transformed. I could even say that I felt "feminized," with the different meanings that that has. I wanted Spielberg to be happy with my performance. I felt a certain pleasure in pleasing him.

L'EXPRESS: *This state of being an actor, is it interesting, troubling?*

F. TRUFFAUT: It's a mixture of frustration and pleasure. The pleasure of having limited responsibility. To lend an appearance, that's all. Not to

From *L'Express*, 13 March 1978. Reprinted by permission of *L'Express*.

make decisions. But the frustration is also large. I never realized at what point actors during the shooting stand apart from everyone. Thus, as we were shooting in a huge hangar in Alabama, I saw apparently important people arriving on the set. Who were they? The insurance people? Bankers? Nobody knew. Rumors circulated. There are a lot of discontented people in a film, but I didn't know. Not as much as that. Certain actors walked up and down all day which made me think of prisoners or pimps. They were unhappy during their awful inactivity. There are idiotic aspects of this métier. A man, very far away, shouts through a megaphone: "The 20 people over there, go back two paces, except Truffaut who must advance three paces." And I had the stupid reflex of being happy and proud to take a step forward, and detach myself from the others. If I was shooting *Day For Night* today, I'd add the private scenes between the actors.

L'EXPRESS: *Has this experience modified your attitude to actors?*
F. TRUFFAUT: Yes. I already had the reputation of not being disagreeable with them. Now, it's true, I'm even more understanding.

L'EXPRESS: *Did you have the status of a "star"?*
F. TRUFFAUT: I had a hairdresser, who was a real bitch. Very funny, a sort of elderly Lana Turner on the wane. A make-up man who never stopped talking about Bernard Fresson under the pretext that I was French. An Italian dresser. That was good. I was like a happy baby having his bottom covered in talc.

L'EXPRESS: *Did a limousine come and fetch you?*
F. TRUFFAUT: The union rules are very strict so that in Wyoming, for example, I didn't have the right to drive to the location in my rented car. I had to wait to be picked up by a car from the production. It was a bit irritating.

L'EXPRESS: *Have you changed your opinion of yourself as an actor?*
F. TRUFFAUT: I find that Spielberg made me smile too much. I told him. Perhaps there are only six smiles in the film, three too many. Otherwise, I think it wasn't a bad idea to have used me because of a certain credibility that I brought to the character.

But we mustn't exaggerate. I'm not playing a real person in the psychological sense. I'm rather a presence. When I saw *Close Encounters*, I remembered the line of Garbo seeing her first film: "I did all that, though I believed I only waited around."

L'EXPRESS: *Do you like the film? Is it close to the way you feel towards science fiction or fantasy?*

F. TRUFFAUT: I could like *Close Encounters of the Third Kind* without being interested in flying saucers just as I like Hitchcock's *The Birds* without being an ornithologist. Besides, even if the film doesn't please me, I feel some solidarity with it because I participated in the adventure. It contains quite strong realistic elements, indispensable if one wants to make the spectators believe in the story, but I can't say I'm interested in UFO's. I'm only interested in sentiments, love stories that may touch me. Meetings that one has in life are so mysterious and so difficult to succeed in that that is enough to satisfy my curiosity. There is science fiction everywhere . . . I think that a film like *Close Encounters of the Third Kind* is a pretext to make a film.

L'EXPRESS: *Was not then* Fahrenheit 451 *a pretext to make a film?*

F. TRUFFAUT: My wish was that there was nothing extraordinary in *Fahrenheit*. One did nothing but burn books. I wanted to film books burning as the burning of people. I don't say that I succeeded, but it was the plan to make a film about the importance of literature. The Spielberg is what I call a big movie of "execution." Example. I read in the screenplay: "An object passes in the sky. A close-up of Lacombe (my character). His hair stands on end." I thought it was just a figure of speech. And, one day, I saw a guy approaching with a sort of saxophone. He was placed at my side, a projector colored my face and the guy plugged in something electric and voila! I actually felt my hair standing on end . . .

L'EXPRESS: *Why was the film shot in that famous hangar far from Hollywood?*

F. TRUFFAUT: I never knew why. It was an abandoned aviation hangar. A sinister place, which cost millions of dollars to fit up, planted in the middle of Mobile, a sad town on the Gulf of Mexico with a lot of poor quarters and empty shops. It is possible that Spielberg wanted to avoid the publicity that dogged the making of *Jaws*.

L'EXPRESS: *Are you interested in special effects?*
F. TRUFFAUT: The most amusing. The remote-controlled camera launched by a computer, without a cameraman . . . Once, I watched how they
made clouds. They let a bomb of white paint go off in a tank of warm
water and filmed the paint that spread in the water at different speeds. If
that movement gives the impression of clouds in the sky . . . Since I visited
the special effects laboratory, I understood that one mustn't ask Spielberg
any questions about my character; that we would be like living silhouettes
in an immense animated film and that it was only necessary to bring to it
one's face and figure.

L'EXPRESS: *Were you impressed by the representation of the creatures that
came from elsewhere?*
F. TRUFFAUT: No, probably because I took part in the shoot. The creatures were small children from Alabama. On the set marvelous things
happened that one doesn't see in the film. The children supported each
other when they were tired. They slept on the ground between scenes.
Unrecognizable in their costumes, they were identical in our eyes. But
they recognized each other. From time to time, we saw them hit each
other, or on the other hand, they would hold each other around the
waist. It was beautiful . . .

L'EXPRESS: *Was the atmosphere of the shoot friendly?*
F. TRUFFAUT: A bit tense towards the end because of the budget which
never stopped rising: 9 million dollars at the start, 11 million when we
arrived in Los Angeles, 15 or 18 million dollars during the shooting.

L'EXPRESS: *Have you ever dreamt for a moment that you would have such
means at your disposal?*
F. TRUFFAUT: Never. No, this type of super-production is too noisy,
and I hate noise. But, what really fascinated me, was the courage of
Spielberg. In France, because of the financial difficulties, we have been
trained to economize. When we find ourselves facing three difficulties
in a shot, we adjust. Spielberg never suppresses anything, never simpli-
fies, he always complicates. In *Close Encounters*, for example, a woman
has three children, another has two. I would have given one child to
one and none to the second!

L'EXPRESS: *Are you the only French director who has a real reputation in the USA?*

F. TRUFFAUT: No, there is also Rohmer, Claude Lelouch, Claude Chabrol, Louis Malle, Alain Resnais, Costa-Gavras . . .

L'EXPRESS: *And you are really not tempted to make a film in America?*

F. TRUFFAUT: In France, it is not ridiculous to make a film without stars. I don't feel less well treated by the industry when I release a film played by unknowns. In America, I was made to feel the difference. I would be in the B league. Meanwhile, each week, I'm offered a script. *Bobby Deerfield* for example. Before Al Pacino and Marthe Keller, they had thought of Paul Newman and Jacqueline Bisset. I was tempted, above all by my liking for the two actors, but race car driving bores me, mainly because of the noise . . .

L'EXPRESS: *Weren't you offered* Bonnie and Clyde?

F. TRUFFAUT: Yes. It was a good script, but not at all for me. It's strange to say, but I don't like gangsters. I was born in Pigalle and, although I didn't suffer from them directly, I saw what they were close up, bad guys who beat up women in the streets. In adapting *Shoot the Piano Player*, I didn't think that I was going to confront that problem. There were gangsters in the David Goodis novel . . . How to get out of it ? To ridicule them, and caricature them a little, but I was not happy with the parody neither. I suffered. I swore never to touch gangsters again. Melville succeeds in treating them like tragic heroes, not me. I realize, finally, that I get no pleasure in putting either politicians or gangsters or people in uniform on the screen. By elimination, I arrived at the point where I only want to film women and children.

L'EXPRESS: *Have you arrived at the point of dedicating one of your films to the face of an actress?*

F. TRUFFAUT: Yes, *Jules and Jim*, to Jeanne Moreau, for example. But, I believe, all the same, that the story comes before everything else. If I choose a big star, then it's a supplementary responsibility. I was in the wrong to cast Catherine Deneuve and Jean-Paul Belmondo in *Mississippi Mermaid*, where they were both used against type. It didn't do any good to their careers . . .

L'EXPRESS: *Are there moments when you draw back from responsibility?*
F. TRUFFAUT: Oh no! But I have confidence in myself in the commercial field. It is rare that one of my films has got its money back only in France. One has to wait for the takings in America and Scandinavia, Germany, Japan . . . It is never disastrous, in any case.

L'EXPRESS: *What effect does the atmosphere of crisis and defeatism of the French cinema have on you?*
F. TRUFFAUT: Not only French. The German cinema is going badly, the Italian also, the British doesn't exist any more. Crisis, what is that? The disproportion between the passion to create on the part of the people in the business and the lack of passion of film-goers, too much gorged on television.

My thoughts are on another point. I think that color has done as much damage to cinema as television. It is necessary to fight against too much realism in the cinema, otherwise it's not an art. At the beginning of the New Wave, in order to exist, we needed to reclaim things, to go back to silent films. We used direct sound and then came color and we forgot to analyze the phenomenon. From the moment that a film is in color, that is shot in the street today, with the sun and the shade and the dialogue covered by the sound of motor bikes, it's not cinema any more. It's not art, it's boring. When all films were in black and white, very few were ugly even when they were lacking in artistic ambition. Now ugliness dominates. Eight films out of ten are as boring as watching a traffic jam.

L'EXPRESS: *But nevertheless you don't shoot in black and white.*
F. TRUFFAUT: Because I can't do otherwise. Whatever the film, it is planned that it will be shown on television one day, and they only buy films in color. Formerly, a film projected in a cinema was exclusively moving images. In a scenario, you added love scenes, a car chase, then exteriors in the mountains, and that was good. Now, it's the contrary. The abundance of action scenes destroys attention. Cinema verité has invaded television news. Fires, the arrest of a gangster, hostage taking . . .

L'EXPRESS: *Is television for you an enemy of film people?*
F. TRUFFAUT: The esthetes, yes, not those who favor characters. For me, the best television writer is—or was—Pagnol.

L'EXPRESS: *Is it true that you have an idea to make a six-hour film for television?*
F. TRUFFAUT: Yes, I will make one. But, rather, 12 hours long. But not while French television is linked to the State. I don't like the idea of working for the government. I've never asked for an advance of the box-office takings. I don't belong to any commission or jury. I don't want the fate of any director or a film of another to depend on me, on my mood or taste.

L'EXPRESS: *Why isn't there political cinema in France?*
F. TRUFFAUT: It doesn't go well with fiction.

L'EXPRESS: *But in Italy, on the other hand, it works.*
F. TRUFFAUT: Because they're dishonest. In any case, easy-going. Honesty is not a quality that inspires creation. It holds you back, rather. In France, we are scrupulous. We are forbidden to cast an American actor, Rod Steiger for example, in the role of Napoleon. That doesn't stop the Italians.

L'EXPRESS: *But Francesco Rosi . . .*
F. TRUFFAUT: Oh! Rosi is their Costa-Gavras! For right or wrong, I believe there is no art without paradox: now in the political film, there is no paradox, because already in the script, it is decided who is good and who is bad. We did not denounce for so many years what was artificial in the cinema of Cayatte to create all of a sudden a neo-cayattism! That is what happened after 1968. One forced filmmakers to give in to blackmail to sprinkle politics on stories that don't need it.

Bad conscience is a strong phenomenon. For me, one of the strongest in the second part of the 20th century. Formerly, one belonged to a class, and then, if one was privileged, one was charitable. Without bad conscience. Bad conscience came with the deportations, the colonial wars, and thanks to television, it allows us to know immediately who is suffering at the other end of the globe.

But a bad conscience is not creative. It never makes a good novel or a good film. It makes us vote more honestly; makes us a better citizen. But it surely doesn't give greater quality to films.

In America, there is a troubling phenomenon . . . the best directors are on the right. The films of Hitchcock, Hawks, Ford, who votes

Republican and who supports the "American presence" in Vietnam, were better than those on the left, most of the time. Besides, there have been awful left-wing Westerns. Americans are perhaps more gifted at exulting war than condemning it.

L'EXPRESS: *Has politics any importance in your life?*
F. TRUFFAUT: Yes. It took me a long time to get interested in it. Finally, I've traveled a lot, and I've come to the conclusion that I have a preference for the socialist monarchies of Scandinavia, because they seem to me countries which have attained real social justice. The presence of a king, a queen creates a fantasy, yet, at the same time, they are very efficient people, who do real work. It's the ministers who are seen on television every day and they're not objects of admiration.

I'm against political prestige. I completely share the ideas of Simenon. I am for the little people against the grand. I don't believe in grand people. Truly . . . The countries which give me the strongest impression of justice are Sweden, Denmark, Norway, and Holland. In Holland you find something unique. The Hollanders born in Holland who are jealous of the advantages that the government has accorded to immigrant workers. I found that a strong sign of civilization. On the other hand, yes, I declare that politicians should be as modest as cleaning women.

L'EXPRESS: *Has something provoked you into this late interest in politics?*
F. TRUFFAUT: With a complete contempt, I thought that politicians were gangsters. I would open a newspaper on the film page. No problem. I knew absolutely nothing that was going on in the world. I was angry on the day that Max Ophuls died because the newspapers only talked about the death of Edouard Heriot. I said to myself: "But who is this person? It's Ophuls who is important."

Afterwards, I was a bit awakened by the Algerian war. In *L'Express*, there were blank pages. Censored articles . . . And then, I signed the Manifesto of 121, because it said that the deserters from the war in Algeria were right and that a part of the population were on their side. Like I joined the Artillery for personal reasons, not for ideological ones, and I equally deserted for personal reasons. Suddenly, I was moved to see this text circulating among intellectuals, and I signed the Manifesto of 121. Following that there was a boycott ordered by Michel Debré. We didn't have the right to appear on television, etc. It didn't last a long time, about a year, a bit like the blacklist.

I don't consider myself on the left, because I'm not militant and because I don't engage myself in political activity, but I'm left-leaning (*gauchisant*), but not on the left (*gauchiste*). What doesn't please me about left-wing intellectuals is that I often get the impression that they are on the left for bad reasons. That is to say, to appear young, to appear revolutionary. For me, there is only one reason to be on the left, because it is more just. That's why I vote socialist.

L'EXPRESS: *Is that a declaration of faith?*
F. TRUFFAUT: Just a statement.

L'EXPRESS: *How do you plan your work?*
F. TRUFFAUT: I practice alternance. Films are hard work. Keeping discipline, an idea all through a film, is tiring. What makes us untired, is to do something opposite. Change activity. If you are fixed on the face of Isabelle Adjani for weeks in *Adèle H*, you relax with 60 children on *Small Change*. You have to pass from one discipline to another different one to rediscover enthusiasm.

L'EXPRESS: *Technically, how do you manage?*
F. TRUFFFAUT: I have files, some of which go back 15 years, but not necessarily thicker than more recent ones. In these 7 or 8 dossiers I have accumulated pieces of paper with bits of dialogue, a lot of newspaper articles. A cutting from a 10-year-old newspaper now yellow is among my files. A man pays a visit to his parents with a young wife. She runs off with her father-in-law. I put this situation in *Day For Night*. Besides this, I go to my office every day. I have a production company. I work like a bureaucrat.

L'EXPRESS: *Do you have a bad conscience when you are not working?*
F. TRUFFAUT: Yes, I have a problem going to the cinema in the afternoon in midweek . . .

L'EXPRESS: *You're never free?*
F. TRUFFAUT: No. I have projects, above all in December . . . It's infuriating to see the year end. The end of a year depresses me terribly.

L'EXPRESS: *How many titles did you prepare last December?*
F. TRUFFAUT: One. *Love on the Run*. The next and last adventure of Antoine Doinel which I'll shoot next June.

L'EXPRESS: *Doesn't all this lack a bit of the unexpected?*
F. TRUFFAUT: Indeed. There is something reasonable about me. I claim nothing; if I'm unemployed one day, I would not declare, "It's scandalous that I can't make a film." You have to have the will. It astonishes me when I see artists demanding things. What can they demand? That their books are in the window, that their films are showing? It is only necessary that others want us. It's like a love affair . . .

L'EXPRESS: *Since you stopped being a critic, do you not have the impression that criticism has lost some ferocity?*
F. TRUFFAUT: Less than its integrity. When I say *Lola Montes* is an admirable film, I believe it. I know the music by heart, and the dialogue. Today, critics often say that a film is admirable, but they wouldn't for the world see it again.

L'EXPRESS: *Doesn't this make you itch to write a review from time to time?*
F. TRUFFAUT: Only when I sense injustice. When Bresson is scorned . . . Sometimes, I take a position against a critic. In *Combat* 30 years ago, I read an article very much against Charles Trenet. "This man who was already there before the war with his carnation in his button-hole . . . there was the war with millions dead, and we now see him again on stage with his hat and carnation in his button-hole . . ." That made me adore Trenet, my favorite singer . . . One expects everybody to change. I like people who are obstinate. I like the faithful.

L'EXPRESS: *Do you think it's possible to be faithful in a film?*
F. TRUFFAUT: It's difficult to foresee if a film will make it. It seems to me that now, contrary to rather diffuse ideas, that the more closed the film, the more it resembles an object, the more chance it has to last. There is a tendency to believe that a film must be open, to serve as a pretext for a discussion with the spectator. That seems to be a hypocritical theory. There is no discussion possible when you present on the screen a slice of life that you have organized and that you want to show to your captives in the dark.

L'EXPRESS: *Do certain of your film objects, with hindsight, inspire you with affection or repulsion?*

F. TRUFFAUT: The only film that I regret having made is *The Bride Wore Black*. I wanted to offer Jeanne Moreau something that didn't resemble any of her other films, but it was badly thought out. Here was a film where the color was an enormous mistake. The theme lacks interest. An apology for idealistic vengeance shocks me in reality. When I saw Robert Enrico's *Le Vieux Fusil* (*The Old Gun*) I experienced a discomfort, but I did the same thing. One doesn't have the right to take vengeance. It is not noble. One betrays something in oneself if one exalts in it.

L'EXPRESS: *What's the next film of yours that we'll see?*

F. TRUFFAUT: *The Green Room.*

L'EXPRESS: *Why green?*

F. TRUFFAUT: Because the other colors were taken. I play the leading role. I've thought about this film for 7 or 8 years . . . the story was difficult to construct, but at the same time, I was attracted to the subject.

L'EXPRESS: *Death?*

F. TRUFFAUT: Rather the faithfulness to death. The idea is this . . . Is it normal that the memory of a death is blurred? I asked myself what would happen to someone who refuses to forget. I've just reached 46, and I've already started to be surrounded by those who have gone. A film like *Shoot the Piano Player* . . . about half the cast have gone. From time to time, the people whom I have lost, I miss as if they have just died. Jean Cocteau for example. So I take one of his records and I listen to it. I listen to his voice in the morning in my bathroom. I miss him . . .

To return to *The Green Room*, I had some not very well-known short stories by Henry James translated by a Russian woman of letters that I know. James, all through his life, was faithful to his dead fiancée. He dedicated a veritable cult to her.

L'EXPRESS: *What do you make of the contradiction between the cult of death and the love of the life?*

F. TRUFFAUT: It's the theme of the film. It is what inspired me to write it with my habitual accomplice, Gruault. I decided to try to write a screenplay, I say try. 5 or 6 years to the making of *The Wild Child* and *Adèle H.* 5 or 6 years equally for *The Green Room*. These screenplays are more careful than others because they are more fragile, more difficult, that make one a little afraid. I don't need to be so careful with an Antoine Doinel film. Once I've got the plot, I work on the dialogue during the shoot when there is much laughter.

L'EXPRESS: *Why did you decide to play in* The Green Room*?*
F. TRUFFAUT: So that the film will be more intimate. Charles Denner would have played it magnificently, but I've just made *The Man Who Loved Women* with him, where we see him throughout the film. Other than Denner, I had no other ideas. It seems to me that if I play the role, I will obtain the same difference as when I write letters in my office, some on the typewriter and others by hand. If you write by hand, it isn't perfect, the writing may be shaky, but it is you, your writing. The typewriter is different. It doesn't seem to me a scornful comparison between actors, because there are the Olivettis with marvelous characters, the Underwoods, the Remingtons have a lot of personality, the portable Japy. I adore typewriters!

L'EXPRESS: *Is it in your role as distributor that you are releasing an unseen Hitchcock?*
F. TRUFFAUT: Yes, *Young and Innocent*. It's not the first time. We gathered five or six friends and we rebought, about 5 years ago, *The Lady Vanishes* and *39 Steps*. Thus the films show from time to time and they don't fall into oblivion. *Young and Innocent* has never been released in France. In the USA, it was titled *The Girl Is Young*. *Young and Innocent* is a very light Hitchcock, without well-known actors, who resemble a little the characters in the novels in the collection *Le Masque*. The film is celebrated by cinéphiles because of one prodigious shot: a man is being sought for murder in a dance hall. We know only that he has a tic in an eye. There is an immense camera movement that moves through the whole dance floor and stops on a blacked-up musician with a tic in the eye . . . the film will be out in May or June.

L'EXPRESS: *What was your relationship with Hitchcock like?*
F. TRUFFAUT: I see him when I go to America. Less since his wife Alma has been ill, but I see him. He always talks about his next film in detail.

More for himself than for anyone else to make sure he is able to tell the plot of his next film shot by shot. If the cinema were a religion, then Hitchcock would be its high priest. He tells also about his arrival in the United States. They told him, "You must be happy. Did you want to go to Hollywood?" and he answered "I'm impatient to enter a big studio and that the heavy doors shut me in." He talks of the Hollywood studios as convents, which is not only an image. Hitchcock is truly a man who locks himself up in cinema, religiously. This impresses me a lot, because it's not my case.

L'EXPRESS: *It's lucky to be, apparently, in any case, balanced and disciplined. You are a very disciplined madman!*
F. TRUFFAUT: Yes, that's true. In any case, nobody could accuse me of having invented much. I think that the world existed before me. I am not important. I know it's false to think like this, but it helps me. For example, I didn't want to have a car accident while shooting *Jules and Jim*, because I knew that the film was very complicated to cut so it was necessary for me to be alive until the final cut. Another time, I told myself, "I can die now." It's a typical case of the importance accorded to the object. I was in Finland when De Gaulle died. I didn't believe it. I said, "I can't believe he's dead. He's busy writing his memoirs." It truly makes no sense to die in the middle of work.

L'EXPRESS: *When you are producer, director, and actor at the same time, which is the heaviest responsibility?*
F. TRUFFAUT: The hardest is the preparation. Fellini showed that magnificently in *8 and a Half*. It's the period when one feels an imposter because you have to solve questions lots of which you don't know the answer. During the shooting, one is faced with really concrete problems that you can really tackle . . .

L'EXPRESS: *What is the final goal?*
F. TRUFFAUT: Go in the direction of fiction. It is more poignant, more intriguing, more interesting. What I'm looking for, in fact, is the truth. There is a paradox in the career of a filmmaker. A novelist prolongs his literary life with conferences, articles, whereas a film director has to pretend to be like a novelist, all his life, even at the moment when he has more of a general view. That's why the films by old people are never

understood. They are always attacked, because they are symbolic. The characters have less depth, but they are very rich films. Only cinéphiles love them.

L'EXPRESS: *Are you thinking of Renoir, of Hitchcock?*
F. TRUFFAUT: Yes, about everyone's last film . . . Dreyer, Hawks . . .

L'EXPRESS: *Do you think about your last films?*
F. TRUFFAUT: Sometimes I imagine that I would be capable of stopping voluntarily, and I dream of a paradise of reading . . . all those books that are waiting to be read. But no. Billy Wilder said: "A film director in retirement becomes president of the jury at the San Sebastian Film Festival."

L'EXPRESS: *In the course of the years, the emotions in your films haven't evolved very much. The fact that man has been to the moon hasn't changed your feelings.*
F. TRUFFAUT: It is almost the contrary. Would I dare to make *Jules and Jim* today? It gave the impression that I was going with the fashion to make a feminist film. At that time, I was struck by the fact that in all the films, even the good ones, if one showed a person loved by two others, one gave the choice to the public of preferring one character to the other. They did not have the idea of an impossible choice. And that's what pleased me, the idea to show, sometimes, that you cannot give a reason for a woman loving two men, both of them good. This idea inspired me. Now, she will be recuperated by feminism, independence, a woman's choice . . . the topical subject that made me want to run away.

I know that this attitude may appear unpleasant. Let's say that my refusal to go with the mode is so deep in me that it makes me want to make films that turn their backs on topical themes which, possibly, could interest me. But I cannot work under pressure, under a menace. And one of the great menaces in 1978 is the fashion.

Truffaut: Twenty Years After

DON ALLEN/1979

TWENTY YEARS AND TWENTY FILMS after launching the
New Wave with his first feature, *Les Quatre Cents Coups*, François Truffaut
talked in Paris recently about the New Wave, the state of the cinema and
himself.

DON ALLEN: *Would it be true to describe your feelings about the New Wave
or what remains of it as pessimistic?*
FRANÇOIS TRUFFAUT: Not really. As you know there are no pessimists
and no optimists, as the moralist said, there are only sad fools and
happy fools. So I don't want to fall into the trap of saying I'm pessimistic. But there has been a lot of talk recently about the New Wave
because it is the twentieth anniversary of the collection of films which
began to appear in 1959. And in all such movements, quite apart from
any artistic considerations, there is the phenomenon of friendship and
individual and group relationships and their inevitable deterioration. In
France the picture is especially complicated, and not only as far as the
cinema is concerned, by the watershed of May 1968. If one thinks of
those of us who used to meet together in one another's homes at a time
when the future seemed to offer happy prospects for everyone, well,
relationships have rather deteriorated since then. Some are in worse
health now than twenty years ago. Some had high hopes which remain
unfulfilled. Friendships have been betrayed. There are a few people
whose beauty increases with age but these are the exceptions. So my
thoughts about the New Wave are not uplifting. Exaggerating a little,

From *Sight and Sound*, Autumn 1979. Reprinted by permission of *Sight and Sound*.

you could say that at the time we were young, handsome, and likeable. And it's anyone's guess whether the last part of the phrase still applies.

DA: *Are the opportunities to make a first film in France any greater than they were twenty years ago for a young person with no money and no connections?*
FT: No, in that in 1959 there was a sudden opening up of possibilities and anyone could make a film. Now the situation has stabilized, but there are still some thirty first films made in France each year by unknowns thanks to the financial support system of loans repayable against the film's future receipts.

The situation in film is more and more like that of a book. It's not very difficult to get a book published. The difficult thing is to get the book into the bookshop window and to get it bought and read. It's the same with the cinema. More and more good films are being made but their fate is less happy than they deserve. It seems to be the case that even the most intelligent and cultured filmgoers frequently prefer a film which is simple but slickly made to one which is intelligent but clumsy. Intellectuals often reject intellectual films made by intellectuals for intellectuals. A case in point in France is Pierre Kast, a highly cultured and literary director who writes articulate and marvellously convincing dialogue and only makes films about intellectuals. And his films are rejected by his intellectual peers, who would rather see, say, a bad, naïve Western than an intelligent one—unless of course it happens to be a masterpiece.

The trouble with many new films, not merely in France, is that their ambition is often greater than the technical expertise with which they are made. In other words, throughout the world there are many uneven films because of the discrepancy between their philosophical or moral intentions, which are too high, and their execution, which is often rather weak. You might call it the crisis of the cinema today.

If you take film production in Hollywood up to the 40s and even the 50s, you have films which give the impression of naiveté on the screen but which were in fact very intelligently made. I think this is true for Hawks's *Big Sky*, *Red River*, and *Airforce*, for instance, films which the intellectual may find naïve and pandering to mass taste and with little concern for psychological conviction, but which were in fact made with a great deal of intelligence behind the camera.

For me, the film that marks the beginning of the period of decadence in the cinema is the first James Bond—*Dr. No*. Until then the role of the cinema had been by and large to tell a story in the hope that the audience would believe it. There had been a few minority films which were parodies of this narrative tradition, but in the main a film told a story and the audience wanted to believe that story. And at this point we might reopen the old polemic about Hitchcock. For years English critics were reluctant to accept that the films Hitchcock made in America were superior to those he made in England. The difference for me lies in the fact that Hitchcock's desire to make the audience believe the story is stronger in his American films than in his English ones.

But the reason I talk of a period of decadence ushered in by the Bond films is that before that parody had been of only minority or snob appeal, but with the Bond films it became a popular genre. For the first time throughout the world, mass audiences were exposed to what amounts as a degradation of the art of cinema, a type of cinema which relates neither to life nor to any romantic tradition but only to other films and always by sending them up. What's more, Hitchcock's career began to suffer from the time of the arrival of the first Bond films, since they were a sort of plagiarized version of *North by Northwest*, his finest thriller. He could not compete with the Bond films and after this he was increasingly obliged to make small-budget films. Perhaps he was also getting rather too old. For instance, had he been ten years younger he might well have made disaster movies. Don't forget he went to America to film *The Titanic* but this was replaced by *Rebecca*.

DA: *Don't you think that disaster movies and super-productions are also in a sense a degradation of cinema—or at least of your concept of cinema?*
FT: No, they mark a return to the origins of cinema, to the first ten or fifteen years. This doesn't worry me at all. The cinema is condemned to produce remakes because too many films are being made and there are too few dramatic situations available. So the whole history of the cinema is studded with remakes, and this is fine as long as the remakes are better than the originals. Six reelers were better than three reelers. There was a loss of quality at the beginning of the talkies but the introduction of sound did not prevent a film like *King Kong* from being very beautifully designed and very ambitious visually. And there are different

mixtures. For example, for a long time it was customary to make period films too respectfully and without the physical explicitness that is to be found in a modern love film. So a remake, say, of *Scarlet Pimpernel*, whose subject matter is very daring, could be very positive if it received a more erotic and sexually convincing treatment.

But the problem now is the need to combat color. How wrong we were to think that color was an improvement and not a handicap.

DA: *Surely this is just part of your general nostalgia?*

FT: No. Perfection in the cinema consists in the knowledge that whatever happens there is a barrier between the film and "reality." Color has removed this last barrier. If there is nothing false in a film, it is not a film—one is in competition with the documentary and the result is very boring. Like much of the film shot for American television, which I find lacking in any fictional dimension, anti-dramatic, over-documentary, and very boring. And a large part of modern cinema is like that.

Color is the enemy. For me it is now much more interesting to construct a flat on the set than to film in a real flat. Because in the studio one at least has the possibility of winning the battle against the ugliness of color, for example by the use of a lot of night shots or by concentrating on the artificial aspects.

DA: *Was the element of color important in* La Chambre Verte?

FT: It wasn't a problem. I didn't shoot either *La Chambre Verte* or *Adèle H* as I would have done in black and white. I avoided showing any streets or period reconstructions or extras in costume. It's in all those areas that danger exists. Also in both these films most of the action takes place at night and night becomes almost part of the décor.

We must return to artifice if we are to stop our films looking like documentaries. I think this is probably what first attracted me to Hitchcock. If there has been one constant thought throughout my life, it is the conviction that the enemy of the sort of cinema that I personally like is the documentary. I have never filmed a documentary in my life and I hope I never do. Not that I cannot admire some of those who have made documentaries, like Marcel Ophuls with *Le Chagrin et la Pitié*. But what first attracted me to the cinema was my love of fiction and what led me to want to make films was the desire to structure a fictional story.

DA: *Are there directors of photography who share your ideas on color?*
FT: There are some who at least ask themselves the same questions. For example, it's not by chance that Nestor Almendros received this year's Academy Award for his work on *Days of Heaven* directed by Terry Malick. And there are five or six excellent directors of photography in France whose aesthetic corresponds to my own. They fight against real light, they try to invent an artificial light and to rediscover the secrets of the old black and white cameramen and apply them to color. That's it in a nutshell.

DA: *And what of the new directors in France? Who do you think is on a level with you and who will one day take your place?*
FT: The one I like best is Eric Rohmer but of course he is of my genera-tion, in fact older than me. But among the newcomers I think one of the best is Claude Miller.

DA: *Who has acted in one of your films.*
FT: I don't think so.

DA: *Yes, he did, in* L'Enfant Sauvage.
FT: Oh yes, that's right, with his wife and baby. He has worked a great deal with me since then, not so much as an assistant but as production manager. I like his films very much. Then there is Jean-François Stévenin, who had a part in *La Nuit Americaine* and also *L'Argent de Poche*. He's a very good actor and director, but I think I prefer him as an actor and any-way he's only directed one film. Someone else who worked with me (and it's not just because they have worked with me that I think they are good!) is Pierre Zucca, who was the stills photographer on *La Nuit Americaine*, and he has made a sophisticated literary/erotic film called *Roberte, Ce Soir*, which is a very beautiful film.

DA: *Can we then talk of an emergence of a Truffaut school?*
FT: No, not at all, because these people are all influenced by other directors than myself. Stévenin is influenced by Bob Rafelson and John Cassavetes and not at all by me. Claude Miller has certainly been influ-enced by Bergman, but if he has points in common with me it's more a question of affinity. For example I share his liking for Bergman, but there is certainly no question of a school, none whatsoever.

DA: *And what about you? Are you not influenced personally by the work of these young directors?*

FT: I think one is influenced above all by what one has seen and experienced before beginning to make films. It is difficult to be influenced after one has begun. It may happen from time to time, but the profound influences appear much earlier, say between the ages of 8 and 15 from the point of view of the emotions and between 15 and 25 from the point of view of style. Afterwards one is constantly refining and polishing one's own personal code, even struggling against it, but it seems to me that one is no longer subject to many other influences.

DA: *But isn't there also the attendant danger of adhering to over-rigid formulae, knowing that when you have solved a problem one way in a particular film you will tend to use the same solution in subsequent films?*

FT: I don't think so entirely. It's true, my films often go in pairs, there is often a film which is like one I made three or four years before, but often I will seek to complicate the problem or to resolve a new difficulty. And sometimes I want to improve something and it turns out worse than my original effort, and then what happens is that a third film emerges which is the synthesis of the previous two. I think that is the way it works.

FT: *You are referring to technical problems?*

DA: I would say aesthetic rather than technical. For example, how can I make a film which follows one straight line with no distractions? For me the question arises in that sort of way. How can I film a short story which appears to last only one hour even if it really lasts one and a half hours? Or on the other hand how can I make a film in which all the characters have the same importance? These are exercises of self-development—part technical, part literary, because they are linked with the development of the script.

DA: *Can you give examples?*

FT: Not really. It's just this alternating pattern between films based on one character and those which attempt to strike a balance between the characters. And for instance the last Antoine Doinel film, *L'Amour en Fuite*, borrows some things from the earlier Doinel films but in its construction it is closer to *L'Homme qui Aimait les Femmes* with its use of the voice-over technique, the commentary, and the attempt to impose a unity on very disparate material.

DA: *Is the commentary important because it conveys a literary tone?*

FT: No, rather a first-person, confidential tone. And the influence here goes back to my childhood and the war years and it is the influence of Sacha Guitry and the charm of the first-person narrative.

DA: *Are you not also influenced in this respect by Henri-Pierre Roché, two of whose novels you have adapted for the cinema? And doesn't* L'Homme qui Aimait les Femmes *also owe a lot to Roché?*

FT: Not too much. I tried to avoid being poetic in this film. I give the hero a scientific occupation and so I wanted him to talk of women from a scientific angle. I was thinking of Howard Hughes, who sent a very famous memo about how Jane Russell's brassiere should be constructed for *Outlaw*—an extraordinary, highly moving memo of about thirty or forty lines, in which he refers to this bra with incredible precision as if it were an airplane engine. So I think it is this scientific aspect I was after in *L'Homme qui Aimait les Femmes*, when Denner says that women's legs are compasses . . . This is not the atmosphere of Roché, who is a "sentimentalist." The sexual dimension in Roché causes no pain. Everything is delightful; everything goes well; it's all too easy. But in my film there is more pain.

But I have certainly been much influenced by Roché. In some respects I'm tempted to describe him as better than Cocteau because he achieves the same effects of "poetic" style more economically. When Cocteau was describing *Antigone* and *Oedipus Rex* he said they were like aerial views of Greece. Roché in my opinion achieves this same effect more simply. What I like about Roché is his prodigious refinement, which enables him to use very few words. One always feels he has the vocabulary of a peasant or of someone who has never read a book or has just learned to read and write—and that is the height of refinement. If we examine his manuscripts we see this was achieved by ruthless cutting in order to achieve the intentionally arid style. I'm no great admirer of my own film version of *Jules and Jim* (I'm pleased it has such a good reputation but it is not as good as its reputation), but it's true that if I listen to the words I still admire the same sentences. Do you remember when they go off to Greece?—"*Ils s'etaient fait faire de clairs costumes pareils*—they had identical light-colored suits made." Only Roché could write that.

And there is a love of things female in general. The refusal to be interested in one type of woman rather than another and the idea that if the personality of the woman is strong then she is to be admired, but above all the refusal to prefer one type of woman to another.

DA: *I wanted to ask you about your fascination with language. You are a "literary" filmmaker who has talked a great deal about language in his films and elsewhere. Could you attempt to evaluate the importance of language in your work and its function as an aid, or obstacle, to communication? One thinks particularly of* Fahrenheit 451, Domicile Conjugal, *and* L'Enfant Sauvage.

FT: It's not something I was particularly conscious of until I read it in articles and reviews. I have been attracted by certain themes and I have sometimes wanted to show books in my films or at least the importance of the written word, but I wouldn't theorize about it. Incidentally it's true that in everyday life I would rather write a letter than telephone. The phone is an aggression. I hate it when it rings. With a letter you can either read it when it arrives or later. You can reply when you wish or not at all. It seems to me more democratic, less authoritarian. So in my films people often communicate by letter. And books are also important.

DA: *On a more personal level, how do you explain your difficulty in mastering the English language?*

FT: I'm very bad at reproducing sounds, but it's a big paradox because after seeing a film twice I know the music by heart, so there is something strange here. I simply can't reproduce the sounds of English. Perhaps because I began late and I didn't continue my formal education for long, so I tended to learn only what seemed vital or useful for earning a living. I never had any of the formal discipline people usually receive during their secondary education. Also I may be rejecting it on a subconscious level. I don't really know but it's very frustrating.

I was very pleased when I first learned to read English. The first thing I read was the collection of memos by David Selznick, which was fantastic. I was so happy because a year before I could not have read it. I haven't tried novels yet, only biographies and books on the cinema. But this represents a considerable progression. But speaking and understanding will always be difficult for me and I shall never completely manage them.

DA: *In your films you frequently depict the lonely man, the outsider. Does this portrayal of the solitude of man represent your own philosophy?*

FT: Not my philosophy of life, but in the cinema there is one kind of film that especially moves me and that is the film with a spoken commentary, for example *Les Enfants Terribles* or *Roman d'un Tricheur* or *Journal d'un Curé de Campagne*. It is as if the director is speaking directly to me and confiding in me as I sit there in the dark. Conversely I have been disappointed even by films by directors I admire when they give the principal character a friend or confidant and my pleasure is spoiled, because even though I want to be interested in the hero, as soon as I know he has a friend I am less interested in what he has to say. An example would be Bresson's *Pickpocket*. I like the film, but the pickpocket has a friend who has guessed his secret and for that reason I cannot completely sympathize with him as I am not that friend. The same is true for my friend Claude Miller's *Dites-lui que je l'Aime*.

So when I am making a film I pay great attention to this aspect. In *L'Homme qui Aimait les Femmes* there is a direct allusion to it in the dialogue when someone says, "You will never see that guy with a man after six p.m." In any case he has no friends, but after six p.m. he will never tolerate the presence of a male. For that reason I think the audience can feel sympathy for, and closeness to, Charles Denner. In *Adèle H* if I had given Adèle a confidant there would not have been a film. The audience is alone with her. That's the feeling I particularly want to get across. It probably comes from my childhood feelings of identification with the hero. I have no time for modern anti-identification theories. If theoreticians and even directors want to indulge in this, O.K., but for my part a film in which the audience identifies with the hero is in no way an inferior genre. On the contrary it's what moves me the most.

I reached the age of eighteen before seeing a single film of Errol Flynn because he only made period films and I never went to see period films. It was some time before I chose films by directors. My first criterion then was the subject matter and I had to work this out from the title. There was always love plus something in the Hollywood films of the period—love plus adventure or love plus western or love plus thriller (my favorite was love plus thriller because there were always characters in raincoats dressed in modern style and therefore it was easy to identify with them.) So I preferred Alan Ladd to Errol Flynn. But I liked Bogart best of all, of course, and the Hollywood psychological films—not that the psychology was particularly refined—and films based on characters with a secret or films with a certain intensity, and above all they had to be modern. The pleasure I experienced was in the company of these rather solitary characters.

There are of course also autobiographical reasons. The fact that I was an only child, as you know, is a very important factor. I think I get on better with people who were only children than with those who had a lot of brothers and sisters. I have a much better understanding of the psychology of the only child. With the only child there is less of the competitive spirit. I personally consider myself very uncompetitive in life. I am part of the French cinema, but the idea of being superior to any other director never occurs to me.

DA: *A criticism which could be levelled at you is that you haven't really made much progress in your films. I know you endorse Renoir's dictum that a filmmaker makes only one film throughout his life and that the rest are merely reworkings of the ideas of that first film. But don't you agree that you do rely too heavily on autobiography, or would you regard this as inevitable? Don't you feel attracted to the idea of a totally new departure?*
FT: It doesn't worry me if it is said that I'm not making any progress. I agree, whatever progress one makes is always very small indeed. One gives the richest part of oneself at the beginning. You could perhaps even say that it's not worth making the cinema your whole career. You should just make say three or four films, which like the first three or four songs of a singer or a songwriter will be the richest. But as it is the activity one most enjoys, one carries on. Even so, I do sometimes make films on difficult subjects . . .

DA: *Like* La Chambre Verte?
FT: Yes, films like that where I "get out of trouble," an expression I prefer to use rather than say I "succeed." Films which turn out fairly well and I can say that perhaps ten years earlier I wouldn't have managed it, I wouldn't have "won the bet." Take the case of *Adèle H.* This was a bet to be won, and it was not lost, but it needed a certain experience in the "business" before one could attempt a film with so few elements. Nor do

I think it would be possible to make *La Nuit Americaine* as a first film. Experience and film-craft are required and one obviously has less film-craft at the beginning of one's career. Sincerity is fine for one's first film, but I don't think one can base one's whole career on sincerity. In addition one needs a little technique and a little skill and of course a little luck. Nothing happens without luck.

DA: *You are still talking of the need to "win bets," as you have been for years now. Nineteen years ago with your second film* Tirez sur le Pianiste *you took a lot of risks. Many people in England consider it your most exciting film even though it was a commercial flop. With very few exceptions, you hardly seemed to have taken a risk since. You now have a solid financial base. Could you not now risk again a new departure, rather than continue, for example, the Antoine Doinel themes and characters, as you do in* L'Amour en Fuite?

FT: I think that the charm of *Pianiste* arises from the element of chance and this same element is also present in *Baisers Volés*. What these two films have in common is the fact that in each case it is impossible to anticipate what will happen next. And it is true that apart from the Doinel films I always know what is going to happen before I begin shooting—at least in general, though of course it is possible to improvise some of the details, because I have confidence in the actors. But during the filming of *Pianiste* I suffered from not knowing what was going to happen to the main character nor what the whole thing was really about. It was a genuine experiment, and it is true that I no longer have the stomach to try something as completely experimental again.

If I were doing *Pianiste* now I would say to myself—Who is that man? What does he want? I would understand the story whereas at the time if I felt like shooting a particular scene I just did it and then followed it with another that was completely different. Though I think this was more acceptable in the climate of the early 60s. I think that if it appeared now it would meet with even greater indifference than it did then. Even so, if there were a thriller that I wanted to film, I would still do it but not with the same naiveté, simply because I no longer have that naiveté. In *Pianiste* there was an element of luck and the charm of Marie Dubois and Nicole Berger and the strangeness of the Aznavour character. It could have been better and it could have been worse, but

I'm not sure it could be done again. When I began *La Mariée était en Noir* I was convinced it would be like *Pianiste* but better. But it turned out worse, though I think the color was a factor here. It was a film that should have been mysterious and yet wasn't. Then I thought I had a good chance with *La Sirène du Mississippi* which was a huge flop—I like the love story but the thriller aspect is very slipshod. On the other hand, it is always a little artificial and absurd to take these American stories and import them into France.

DA: *Will you go on asking the same questions?*
FT: I've no idea. I have some films which I haven't yet made and which I certainly will make. For example, I should like to make a love story against a background of classical music. I should also like to make a film on France under the Occupation. I shall have to check my files and meet some Jews who worked clandestinely in Paris during the war and who will tell me of their experiences. I am also meeting some young musicians from the Conservatoire, and according to the richness of these conversations I will decide what to film next. Perhaps I will take the subject which needs least research.

DA: *So you will need this foundation of "truth" and real life? From this point of view you haven't changed in twenty years. And likewise you remain socially and politically uncommitted?*
FT: Yes, partly for autobiographical reasons. I don't feel one hundred per cent French and I don't know the whole truth about my origins. I've never tried to obtain a voting card so I can't vote. I would feel I was performing a very artificial act if I voted, as if I were acting a part. So I feel no attachment to France and could well finish my days in a different country. Just as the notion of patriotism has no hold on me, so too when people try to explain their religion to me, I remain skeptical and feel they cannot be sincere—which is stupid because they are. I just cannot hold their beliefs. My religion is the cinema. I believe in Charlie Chaplin, etc. As for politics I think its importance has been greatly exaggerated and over-valued for the last ten years. Politics for me simply amounts to doing the housework: if the dust needs getting rid of this morning, we get rid of it—without talking about it: if the ashtrays need emptying we empty them, but it is not the most important task

of the day. It's necessary, but if it becomes the sum total of our conversation or of our day, then it is folly. The same applies to politics. Politicians do not deserve their star status. They should simply be modest and efficient charwomen.

DA: *So politics doesn't change people's lives or the structures of society?*
FT: Only very slowly. And the slower it is the more effective it is. Changes are not spectacular. What's more, if it is felt that in twenty years' time a film with a political content will give a clearer picture of the society in which it is made than a non-political film, this is quite untrue. Some of the sophisticated Hollywood comedies say as much about America years ago as any films aimed at denouncing some particular social abuse. The idea that one must strive to reflect the society in which one lives is false—because one will do so in any case, intentionally or not. Salvador Dali gave painters this advice. Above all don't worry about being "modern" because unfortunately, whatever you do, you will be.

There is a lot of pressure on film-makers from the media to get them to introduce a political dimension, even an artificial one, into their work. It is very important to resist these pressures. Film-making should be a pleasure, not a duty. We must be free to follow our instincts in our choice of subject. You don't make a film to please a particular section of public opinion. You make a film for your own pleasure and in the hope that the audience will share it. If film-making became a duty I would do something else. The number one question for me is how one spends one's time. One must give oneself a timetable that one likes, which is why I chose the cinema. Otherwise I might perhaps write. But the most important thing for me is to be free of all constraints.

This political blackmail of recent years is a negative and disagreeable aspect of our times. Fortunately it's coming to an end—cruelly. Thanks to the paradox of history; thanks to the fact that the Ayatollah Khomeini is worse than the former Shah of Iran; thanks to the fact that the Vietnamese have invaded Cambodia and the Chinese have supported the Cambodians; thanks to all these gory paradoxes it is clear that people cannot be pushed in one single direction. Life is full of paradoxes and the cinema must reflect these paradoxes. And in so-called political films there is no life because there are no paradoxes. The film director goes to work

knowing in advance who is the corrupt police inspector, who is the dishonest property developer, who is the brave young reporter, etc. For a
long time in France André Cayatte was the only director to make this
type of film. Since 1968 there has been a vogue for what I call "neo-
Cayattism"—which, as a spectator, I absolutely refuse to see and, as a
film-maker, I absolutely refuse to practice.

How Truffaut's *The Last Metro* Reflects Occupied Paris

ANNETTE INSDORF / 1981

" I ALWAYS THOUGHT of making this film," said François Truffaut as he discussed the origins of *The Last Metro*, his affectionate story of a theater company in German-occupied Paris which opens Wednesday at the Coronet. "At the beginning of my career, I couldn't do it, because it was too close to *The 400 Blows*, not in terms of the occupation, but my own age at that time."

Having been reluctant to make two consecutive movies about a small boy, Mr. Truffaut said, "Then I thought of doing a love story about the occupation, but when I saw *The Sorrow and the Pity* (Marcel Ophuls's documentary about French complicity in the occupation), I said to myself, "How can I make a fiction film that could measure up to a documentary like *The Sorrow and the Pity*?"

"Then, of course," said the 48-year-old director, "the subject came into vogue, and there was a whole series of French films about the occupation—like *Lacombe, Lucien, Les Violons du Bal*, and *Mr. Klein*. So I said again, 'This is not the right moment.'"

After the wave subsided, Mr. Truffaut said, he was stimulated by actor Jean Marais's autobiography as well as other documents by and about theater people during the occupation. Actors' memoirs, research, and the director's own experiences as a child in wartime France provided the details that make up *The Last Metro*, Mr. Truffaut said in a discussion that covered not only the origins of *The Last Metro* and the film's muted but

From the *New York Times*, 8 February 1981. Copyright © 1981 by the New York Times Co. Reprinted with permission.

unflinching depiction of anti-Semitism, but also Mr. Truffaut's reassessment of the concept of the director as auteur.

As the closing night selection of the New York Film Festival last October, *The Last Metro* received a standing ovation and critical praise. The film comes to New York as the director's 19th feature and France's nominee for an Academy Award as the best foreign film.

In it, Lucas Steiner (Heinz Bennent), a respected German-Jewish stage director, is forced to go underground amid mounting anti-Semitism in 1942; and his wife, Marion (Catherine Deneuve), takes over their theater with a firm hand. The problems she must surmount include the subtle threats of the pro-Nazi drama critic Daxiat (Jean-Louis Richard), the romantic appeal of her new leading man, Bernard (Gerard Depardieu), and the curfew which requires their curtain to come down in time for the night's last subway service. Thus, the limitations of war define the possibilities of theater.

"The script is nourished by real things," explained Mr. Truffaut. "It shows the resourcefulness and ruses of daily life during the occupation. War films usually have big events and heroic actions; *The Last Metro* is interesting, I suppose, because of its small details. It's almost as if seen by a child because the things that struck me at the time are woven into the film." Of equal importance for Mr. Truffaut is the contribution of co-scenarist and assistant director Suzanne Schiffman, who was also a child in 1942. "She brought in more dramatic elements. After all, her mother was deported and never came back," he added.

The wartime experience of Mr. Truffaut, who is not Jewish, were less traumatizing, but the deportation of his uncle to a small concentration camp (for politics rather than religion) feeds into *The Last Metro*. On the day of his arrest, this uncle prevented a Resistance comrade from suffering a similar fate by quietly signaling not to acknowledge him at their rendezvous. "We simply transposed the locale from a train station to a church," said the director about the scene of Bernard's close call with the Gestapo.

Mr. Truffaut recalled the occupation as a period when "everything was paradoxical. We were told to be honest, while surrounded by examples of the dishonesty needed to survive. For example, without food tickets, we would have starved. We had false tickets—badly made, obviously—so children were sent to the grocers: 'They'll close their eyes and wouldn't dare send back kids,' we said. I'm sure that my profound wariness of all certitudes stems from this period."

Mr. Truffaut admitted that "had *The Last Metro*—which is not easy to categorize—come out a few years ago, it would have been attacked for being very tolerant of the characters and expressing sympathy for everyone, including those 'show people' who continued to perform during the war. But now," he added from behind a cloud of cigar smoke, "since Mao's death, the invasion of Afghanistan, and the upheaval in Iran, it's once again possible to accept the idea that life is paradoxical."

His vision of filmmaking is a far cry from the didactic social commentary that has characterized much of European cinema: "After '68, in Europe," he said, "politics were overestimated. You kept hearing the slogan, 'everything is political'—which I find absurd."

In *The Last Metro*, this line is uttered by the Nazi sympathizer Daxiat (based on an actual critic of the extreme right) as a justification for ridding France of the Jews. One of the few villains in Mr. Truffaut's sympathetic body of work, this character illustrates the filmmaker's premise that there was often more to fear from the pro-Nazi French than from the Germans.

"That's why there are almost no Germans in the film. One of the most monstrous things during the war was the *Rafle de Veld'hiv*, and it was the French who did it," he elaborated, referring to the roundup of 13,000 Jews by the Paris police on July 16, 1942. (This event, which facilitated deportation to concentration camps from Paris's Velodrome d'Hiver, is also recreated in Joseph Losey's *Mr. Klein*.)

Despite *The Last Metro*'s sensitivity to the plight of Jews in wartime France, anti-Semitism is hardly its main theme. While the film calls attention to the fact that actors had to have an Aryan Certificate in order to act on stage or screen, it does not dwell, for example, on the point that Jews had to ride in the last car of the train. Mr. Truffaut's contention that "this film is not concerned merely with anti-Semitism but intolerance in general" is evidenced by the fact that *The Last Metro* encompasses a homosexual director (Jean Poiret) and a lesbian designer (Andrea Ferreol) with great ease.

Why, then, include these characters whose sexual orientation is not an issue? "Suzanne and I observed that the collaborationist, extreme-right press condemned Jews and homosexuals in the same breath. The French pro-Nazis had a very naive image of Germany—virile male strength. It's absurd to look only at films like Visconti's *The Damned*: sure, there were lots of homosexuals in the SS. But for the Nazis, the weak were 'female' in a pejorative sense. Hence, the phobia against homosexuals. It always pops up in reviews of the collaborationist newspaper *Je Suis Partout* (I Am Everywhere): you read, for instance, 'a play that reeks of Jewishness and effeminacy.'"

In *The Last Metro*, this accusation is leveled by Daxiat at the Steiners' productions. The role of Lucas Steiner—a Jewish director who is clearly not effeminate—was, in fact, a source of controversy when it was first given to Mr. Bennent, a German actor. Prior to the opening of the film, Mr. Truffaut voiced doubts about casting a German (who had just incarnated an eager Nazi in *The Tin Drum*) as a Jew. But afterward, he admitted, "It's one of those problems that one creates for oneself. Bennent is a great actor, and I'm no longer afraid that he won't be plausible as a Jew—even in Germany. In France, no one recognizes him from Schlondorff's films. They simply ask, 'Who's this great actor?' "

His role took shape from speculation about a celebrated French performer: "The Germans wanted Louis Jouvet to stay in France and stage German plays. But Jouvet took his troupe to Portugal and then South America. Our point of departure was, what if Jouvet had remained, hidden in the cellar of his theater?"

Turning from discussing film in particular to discussing film in general, Mr. Truffaut, the former critic whose provocative articles for *Cahiers du Cinema* in the 1950s helped create the cult of the auteur, said he now finds that the director needs to be demythologized. "There's an entire vocabulary that has to be abandoned, like 'direction of actors.' As a director, I'm ashamed of this phrase. I struggle against the very word— I direct no one. I'm not a captain! I point them toward what is good for them or for the film."

"When you switch from critic to filmmaker," he continued with intensity, "you can't use the same expressions—and certainly not *cinema d'auteur*. The terms you could manipulate as a critic become shocking in the mouth of a director. Take *hommage*, for example: now you can copy anything, plagiarize, and call it homage. We have to stop talking of these things. Influence is a question of spirit, not quotation."

In Mr. Truffaut's opinion, Americans have a stronger sense of concept than the French. As an example, he proposed that if a French director were to recount the story of his next film, "He would tell it as if it had never been told before, since the beginning of cinema history. An American director would simply answer the questions, 'Who is the girl? Who is the boy? Who are the actors? What is the background?' as if it's understood that it's always the same story, only the background changes," he added with a laugh.

Despite his role in Steven Spielberg's *Close Encounters of the Third Kind*, the American cinema is still unfamiliar territory for Mr. Truffaut. To the question of whether he would consider directing an American film, he responded, "The place is not important. The only question is the language—French or English. Stanley Kubrick makes American films without setting foot in America! If I had four or five properties, and one would be as logical in English as in French, I'd say maybe it could be in English. But *The Last Metro*, for example, could never have been made in English."

The notion of planning four or five projects at a time may seem like a risky juggling act, but Mr. Truffaut has always performed it nimbly. "I work in cycles, and need four or five projects," he said. "The order can change but it reassures me to have a few. While shooting one film, I like to take notes to serve another. Otherwise, when a film is over, you feel too drained."

Now that *The Last Metro* has immersed him in the world of the theater, would Mr. Truffaut consider directing plays? Shaking his head, he declined: "If you tell me a story—that yesterday you met a boy, for example—I see the different scales while you're talking: a two-shot here, a close-up there. I still see stories in terms of shots." With obvious affection, he said, "Filmmaking is a very special discipline."

INDEX

CONVERSATIONS WITH FILMMAKERS SERIES
PETER BRUNETTE, GENERAL EDITOR

The collected interviews with notable modern directors, including

Robert Aldrich • Woody Allen • Pedro Almodóvar • Robert Altman • Theo Angelopolous • Ingmar Bergman • Bernardo Bertolucci • Tim Burton • Jane Campion • Frank Capra • Charlie Chaplin • The Coen Brothers • Francis Ford Coppola • George Cukor • Brian De Palma • Clint Eastwood • Federico Fellini • John Ford • Terry Gilliam • Jean-Luc Godard • Peter Greenaway • Howard Hawks • Alfred Hitchcock • John Huston • Jim Jarmusch • Elia Kazan • Buster Keaton • Stanley Kubrick • Akira Kurosawa • Fritz Lang • Spike Lee • Mike Leigh • George Lucas • Sidney Lumet • Joseph L. Mankiewicz • Roman Polanski • Michael Powell • Satyajit Ray • Jean Renoir • Martin Ritt • Carlos Saura • John Sayles • Martin Scorsese • Ridley Scott • Steven Soderbergh • Steven Spielberg • George Stevens • Oliver Stone • Quentin Tarantino • Andrei Tarkovsky • Lars von Trier • Liv Ullmann • Orson Welles • Billy Wilder • John Woo • Zhang Yimou • Fred Zinnemann

3/10/08